STOCKTON - BI

LEARNING CENTRE

COLLEGE

823 AUS

KU-220-184

MACMILLAN MASTE

MANSFIELD PARK
BY JANE AUSTEN

MACMILLAN MASTER GUIDES

General Editor: James Gibson

Published:
JANE AUSTEN: **PRIDE AND PREJUDICE** Raymond Wilson
        EMMA Norman Page
        MANSFIELD PARK Richard Wirdnam
ROBERT BOLT: **A MAN FOR ALL SEASONS** Leonard Smith
EMILY BRONTË: **WUTHERING HEIGHTS** Hilda D. Spear
GEOFFREY CHAUCER: **THE PROLOGUE TO THE CANTERBURY
        TALES** Nigel Thomas and Richard Swan
CHARLES DICKENS: **GREAT EXPECTATIONS** Dennis Butts
        HARD TIMES Norman Page
GEORGE ELIOT: **MIDDLEMARCH** Graham Handley
        SILAS MARNER Graham Handley
OLIVER GOLDSMITH: **SHE STOOPS TO CONQUER** Paul Ranger
THOMAS HARDY: **FAR FROM THE MADDING CROWD**
        Colin Temblett-Wood
CHRISTOPHER MARLOWE: **DOCTOR FAUSTUS** David A. Male
GEORGE ORWELL: **ANIMAL FARM** Jean Armstrong
WILLIAM SHAKESPEARE: **MACBETH** David Elloway
        A MIDSUMMER NIGHT'S DREAM
        Kenneth Pickering
        ROMEO AND JULIET Helen Morris
        THE WINTER'S TALE Diana Devlin

Forthcoming:
GEOFFREY CHAUCER: **THE MILLER'S TALE** Michael Alexander
T. S. ELIOT: **MURDER IN THE CATHEDRAL** Paul Lapworth
E. M. FORSTER: **A PASSAGE TO INDIA** Hilda D. Spear
WILLIAM GOLDING: **THE SPIRE** Rosemary Sumner
THOMAS HARDY: **TESS OF THE D'URBERVILLES** James Gibson
HARPER LEE: **TO KILL A MOCKINGBIRD** Jean Armstrong
        THE METAPHYSICAL POETS Joan van Emden
ARTHUR MILLER: **THE CRUCIBLE** Leonard Smith
GEORGE BERNARD SHAW **ST JOAN** Leonee Ormond
WILLIAM SHAKESPEARE: **HAMLET** Jean Brooks
        HENRY IV PART ONE Helen Morris
        JULIUS CAESAR David Elloway
        KING LEAR Francis Casey
        OTHELLO Christopher Beddowes
        TWELFTH NIGHT Edward Leeson
RICHARD SHERIDAN: **THE RIVALS** Jeremy Rowe
        THE SCHOOL FOR SCANDAL Paul Ranger
JOHN WEBSTER: **THE DUCHESS OF MALFI/THE WHITE DEVIL**
        David A. Male

Also published by Macmillan

MACMILLAN MASTER SERIES

Mastering English Literature R. Gill
Mastering English Language S. H. Burton
Mastering English Grammar S. H. Burton

MACMILLAN MASTER GUIDES

MANSFIELD PARK

BY JANE AUSTEN

RICHARD WIRDNAM

MACMILLAN

© Richard Wirdnam 1985

All rights reserved. No reproduction, copy or transmission
of this publication may be made without written permission.

No paragraph of this publication may be reproduced, copied
or transmitted save with written permission or in accordance
with the provisions of the Copyright Act 1956 (as amended).

Any person who does any unauthorised act in relation to
this publication may be liable to criminal prosecution and
civil claims for damages.

First edition 1985

Published by
MACMILLAN EDUCATION LTD
Houndmills, Basingstoke, Hampshire RG21 2XS
and London
Companies and representatives
throughout the world

Printed in Hong Kong

British Library Cataloguing in Publication Data
Wirdnam, Richard
Mansfield Park by Jane Austen.
1. Austen, Jane. Mansfield Park
I. Title II. Austen, Jane. Mansfield Park
823'.7   PR4034.M33
ISBN 0-333-37429-0 Pbk
ISBN 0-333-39472-0 Pbk export

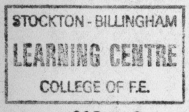

STOCKTON - BILLINGHAM

LEARNING CENTRE

COLLEGE OF F.E.

823 AUS

To Susan

The great charm, however, of English scenery is the moral feeling that seems to pervade it. It is associated in the mind with ideas of order, of quiet, of sober, well-established principles, of hoary usage, and reverend custom. Everything seems to be the growth of ages of regular and peaceful existence. The old church of remote architecture ... the parsonage, a quaint, irregular pile, partly antiquated, but repaired, and altered in the tastes of various ages and occupants ... the antique family mansion, standing apart in some little rural domain, but looking down with a protecting air on the surrounding scene; all these common features of English landscape evince a calm and settled security, and hereditary transmission of home-bred virtues and local attachments, that speak deeply and touchingly for the moral character of the nation.

WASHINGTON IRVING

CONTENTS

GENERAL EDITOR'S PREFACE

The aim of the Macmillan Master Guides is to help you to appreciate the book you are studying by providing information about it and by suggesting ways of reading and thinking about it which will lead to a fuller understanding. The section on the writer's life and background has been designed to illustrate those aspects of the writer's life which have influenced the work, and to place it in its personal and literary context. The summaries and critical commentary are of special importance in that each brief summary of the action is followed by an examination of the significant critical points. The space which might have been given to repetitive explanatory notes has been devoted to a detailed analysis of the kind of passage which might confront you in an examination. Literary criticism is concerned with both the broader aspects of the work being studied and with its detail. The ideas which meet us in reading a great work of literature, and their relevance to us today, are an essential part of our study, and our Guides look at the thought of their subject in some detail. But just as essential is the craft with which the writer has constructed his work of art, and this is considered under several technical headings - characterisation, language, style and stagecraft.

The authors of these Guides are all teachers and writers of wide experience, and they have chosen to write about books they admire and know well in the belief that they can communicate their admiration to you. But you yourself must read and know intimately the book you are studying. No one can do that for you. You should see this book as a lamppost. Use it to shed light, not to lean against. If you know your text and know what it is saying about life, and how it says it, then you will enjoy it, and there is no better way of passing an examination in literature.

JAMES GIBSON

ACKNOWLEDGEMENTS

Cover illustration: *Richmond Hill and Bridge* by J.M.W. Turner. Courtesy of the Trustees of the British Museum.

1 LIFE AND BACKGROUND

1.1 THE LIFE

Jane Austen's life can be summarised in very few words. She was born on 16 December 1775 in the village of Steventon, Hampshire – one of eight children. Her father was the rector of the village, and her childhood was spent in the rectory. She was sent away to school for a brief period, but most of her education was received from her father, who was a fine scholar. At an early age she began to write short pieces to amuse other members of the family, and by 1790 had completed *Love and Freindship*, an example of her ability to parody the worst kinds of popular fiction. By 1797 she was working on the novel that was to become *Pride and Prejudice*, and *Sense and Sensibility* was also begun at about this period while Jane was visiting the popular spa town of Bath. She made many other visits to friends and relations, particularly to the home of her brother Edward at Godmersham Park in Kent. By 1798 she had started writing *Susan*, which was published posthumously as *Northanger Abbey*.

In 1801 Mr Austen announced his decision to retire to Bath – news which Jane received with dismay, for she was attached to the countryside of southern England, and although towns and cities appear in her novels, they are not generally viewed in a sympathetic way. From 1801 until 1809, when she returned to Hampshire permanently, Jane wrote very little, and it appears to have been an unsettled period in her life. She spent her summers at seaside resorts like Sidmouth and Lyme Regis, and it was at one of these that she encountered the young man whose early death may have ended the only serious romantic attachment in her life. The death of Mr Austen, in 1805, left Jane, her sister Cassandra and their mother in a somewhat precarious financial position, but they were assisted by other members of the family, and by 1807 they were lodging in Southampton.

Jane must have been overjoyed when Edward offered his mother and sisters a house at Chawton, not far from her childhood home at Steventon. It meant a return to the life of a country village which provided the material of so much of Jane Austen's fiction. During the years spent at Chawton she revised her earlier fiction, and wrote *Mansfield Park*, *Emma* and *Persuasion*. The publication of her novels brought acclaim from many sources, but Jane Austen never became a celebrity, preferring to remain an anonymous writer, even to close friends. *Mansfield Park* was written between 1811 and 1813, and published, in three volumes, in 1814.

In 1817 Jane's health began to give cause for concern. We now believe she suffered from Addison's disease, which causes general weakness, and she was unable to complete her novel *Sanditon*. She was moved to Winchester to ensure adequate medical attention, but died on 18 July 1817 in the arms of Cassandra. Jane Austen was buried in Winchester Cathedral, but her real monument is the six novels completed during her lifetime, which have remained some of the most widely read in the language.

The world into which Jane Austen was born was that of the gentry - a kind of upper-middle class - and it may seem, in modern eyes, a somewhat narrow and provincial one. Birth was the usual criterion for being a member of the gentry, but it was a mixed group. At the top of the social class were baronets like Sir Thomas Bertram - these were also classed as minor members of the aristocracy - while at the bottom were smaller landowners. In between might be found educated clergymen, lawyers, naval officers - often the younger sons of landowners - and some wealthy tradespeople. All these might be classed as 'gentlemen' - just as the anonymous author of *Sense and Sensibility* could term herself 'a lady'. The gentry as a class made its money from owning land, and it tended to be rather conservative in outlook, living in the country and believing in the doctrines of the Church of England. It is hardly surprising that Jane Austen, a clergyman's daughter, shared these beliefs, as well as certain assumptions about society as a whole, but while she is a daughter of her class she is not a complacent one, and is quite prepared to question some of its attitudes in her novels.

The life of the country gentry centred on the family, and Jane Austen's was large and closely knit. Her letters to Cassandra are full of family gossip, and at times it becomes almost impossible to keep track of all her various nephews and nieces. Through members of her family, Jane Austen kept in touch with world events, and visiting them gave her an opportunity to travel. The careers of her brothers provided her with a great deal of information that was to find its way into the novels. Edward Austen was adopted by a wealthy, childless couple, and after taking their family name of Knight, inherited estates in Kent and Hampshire. From conversations with him Jane would have learnt how land and houses might be improved, and what ought to be done for the welfare of tenant farmers. In *Mansfield Park* we catch glimpses of how an estate is run, and in Sir Thomas, Henry Crawford and Mr Rushworth we see three very different examples of landowners. James and Henry Austen both became clergymen – although the latter tried several other careers first – and with a father in the profession as well it is no wonder that so many details about ordination and the duties of an incumbent find their way into the novel. Frank and Charles Austen both entered the navy, and were successful, eventually becoming admirals. Some of Frank's ships are mentioned in *Mansfield Park*, and knowledge of prize money and foreign settings came in useful when Jane started to create the character of William Price – Fanny's sailor brother. Charles bought his sisters topaz crosses out of his prize money, and even this detail finds its way into the novel. From her letters it is clear that Jane was also well-informed about the progress of the war against France, the American war of 1812 and many other contemporary events. Her cousin Eliza's first husband – a French nobleman – had been guillotined during the Revolution, and Warren Hastings, at one time virtual governor of India, was a family friend.

Like Fanny Price – who questions Sir Thomas about the slavery issue – Jane Austen was not uninterested or uninformed about important issues, and yet, much of her knowledge remains on the periphery of the world of the novels, for in them, the world of the gentry becomes only that portion accessible to women – the domestic affairs of '3 or 4 Families in a Country Village'. Men are never depicted without the presence of women, and their purely masculine concerns remain unexplored – political matters, for example, are not discussed in the drawing-room at Mansfield.

1.2 JANE AUSTEN'S WRITING OF NOVELS

Jane Austen's choice of subject matter was deliberate, and consisted of those areas of the country life of the gentry she understood best. An examination of *Mansfield Park* reveals that the everyday affairs of the house are given far more space than so-called 'dramatic' events. Maria's elopement and Tom's illness are narrated briefly, while an evening spent at the Parsonage playing cards is given a whole chapter. Sir Thomas's trip to Antigua, or William's naval exploits would have been recounted in full to the Bertram family, but we, as readers, are given only snippets – our attention being focused on the various reactions of the listeners. The most important incidents in the novel are a visit to a neighbour's house, the rehearsals for a play, a ball and Fanny's visit to her parent's home in Portsmouth. These are a fair indication of the kind of social life Jane Austen would have led. Her brothers might travel unaccompanied to school or university, pursue their chosen careers and go hunting in all weathers, but Jane and Cassandra were unable to enjoy an equal degree of freedom. They visited friends and relations (accompanied of course!), danced at occasional balls and walked when the lanes were not muddy. They managed to attend concerts and plays while staying at Bath, or in London with brother Henry, spend their money in shops and make summer excursions to the seaside. These are the only variations Jane Austen allows her heroines, and in *Mansfield Park* Fanny Price's existence is confined further by the ill-health of her aunt, and on only two occasions does she travel outside the park.

Jane Austen's letters record her major preoccupations, and those of the ladies in *Mansfield Park* – sewing (for themselves and the poor), reading to themselves or out loud for the entertainment of others, drawing and painting, music-making, letter-writing, light gardening and supervising the smooth running of the household. It is from ordinary activities like these that the novels are created.

But if that was all the novels were about – the domestic life of the gentry – we would not be concerned with them today, or we would dismiss them as somewhat limited fragments of social history. It is Jane Austen's artistic genius that transforms everyday occurrences into a work of art. She was praised for her skill with a needle, and her novels are constructed with as much love and care as her needlework. In later life Jane was to give useful advice to a niece who was writing a novel, and it is clear from her comments that she had given a considerable amount of thought to the kind of fiction she wanted to create.

In her early works Jane Austen's aims had been to entertain other members of the family, and to parody the over-sentimental novels of the period. Later she was to ridicule the Gothic novel – a kind of horror story designed to make its readers shudder. This first period of her career led to the early versions of *Pride and Prejudice*, *Sense and Sensibility* and *Northanger Abbey*. We cannot be certain what these were like, but they may well have been written in letter form, and the elements of parody have been much stronger. When Jane Austen returned to writing fiction in the years following her arrival at Chawton, it was with a more mature approach, a firmer sense of how a novel should be constructed and what should be its subject matter. During the Chawton years Jane Austen worked steadily at her fiction in a quiet and meticulous way - slotting it into her daily routine and looking to her immediate family for criticism. She wrote on single sheets of paper, so that they might be quickly concealed if a stranger disturbed her. Anonymity allowed her to remain an undetected observer of the life going on around her, and she was concerned when Henry inadvertently revealed the identity of his famous sister. Jane was in no way ashamed of her achievements, but she had realised where the material of her fiction was to be found, and wished to remain Miss Jane Austen or Aunt Jane. Fame might have destroyed vital links with the world she knew best.

The tone of the novelist commenting on the work of a nephew is that of an artist sure of her limitations and strengths:

> What should I do with your strong, manly, spirited Sketches, full of Variety and Glow? - How could I possibly join them on to the little bit (two Inches wide) of Ivory on which I work with so fine a Brush, as produces little effect after much labour?

We can detect the same tone in a reply to an invitation from the secretary of the Prince of Wales to write an historical romance:

> You are very very kind in your hints as to the sort of composition which might recommend me at present, and I am fully sensible that an historical romance, founded on the House of Saxe Cobourg, might be much more to the purpose of profit or popularity than such pictures of domestic life in country villages as I deal in. But I could no more write a romance than an epic poem. I could not sit seriously down to write a serious romance under any other motive than to save my life; and if it were indispensable for me to keep it up and never relax into laughing at myself or other people, I am sure I should be hung before I had finished the first chapter. No, I must keep to my own style and go on in my own way; and though I may never succeed again in that, I am convinced that I should totally fail in any other.

Because of their subject matter, Jane Austen's novels have been condemned by some readers because they seem unimportant and even trivial, yet this is not a fair judgement. All of us feel the urge for excitement and adventure, and novels with dramatic events in them provide a form of escape if we find ourselves stuck in an apparent rut. Yet few of us will ever lead the kind of lives we dream for ourselves, and Jane Austen helps us to accept this because she shows that the apparently trivial is not insignificant. All our acts have a moral significance for ourselves and those around us, especially when we are concerned with those emotions and desires that are timeless – love, prejudice, greed, jealousy. It is upon these basic emotions and patterns of behaviour that *Mansfield Park* is founded.

2 SUMMARIES
AND
CRITICAL COMMENTARY

Chapter 1

Mansfield Park is the home of Sir Thomas and Lady Bertram and their children. Lady Bertram has two sisters. The eldest, Mrs Norris, is married to the rector of Mansfield, and the younger, Mrs Price, to a lieutenant of marines. The Prices have too little money for bringing up their numerous children, so on the instigation of Mrs Norris, much thought is given to the question of bringing one of the children, Fanny, to Mansfield, to be educated with the Bertram girls.

Commentary

In the opening paragraph we are shown three very different marriages, and the results of them – these should be remembered when the whole issue of Fanny's possible marriage to Henry Crawford is raised later in the novel. Notice how quickly Jane Austen introduces us to the characters of the three people directly concerned in Fanny Price's future. Sir Thomas is solid, rational and full of dignity, but rather cold and austere – his language pompous and formal. Mrs Norris is full of bustling self-importance, but has no intention of spending her own money, or giving up any of her own comforts – 'nobody knew better how to dictate liberality to others'. Lady Bertram is indolent to the point of apathy – her tranquil world is seldom disturbed by strong feelings, and her only concern in the future welfare of Fanny is whether the latter will tease her lap-dog.

Chapter 2

Fanny arrives at Mansfield, and is introduced to the Bertram children – Tom, Edmund, Maria and Julia. She finds difficulty in adjusting to her new home, but, with Edmund's assistance, begins to fit into the Mansfield way of life. Maria and Julia are appalled by Fanny's ignorance, and we learn about the kind of education they have received. Sir Thomas continues to take an interest in the rest of the Price family – particularly Fanny's favourite brother, William, who becomes a midshipman in the navy.

Commentary

Jane Austen skilfully depicts the fears and uncertainties of a timid ten-year-old at finding herself in a great country house. If, later in the novel, we are tempted to despise Fanny for not being a more demonstrative person, then this chapter should help us to understand how her character was formed. Jane Austen always portrays children skilfully, but this is the only occasion in the major novels where we see the world through a child's eyes. Edmund's kindness quickly establishes him as a sympathetic character, and the last sentence of the chapter implants in the reader's mind the notion that Fanny's gratitude will develop into something more substantial.

Chapter 3

Five years have passed since Fanny's arrival, and the death of Mr Norris causes much discussion on who is to be his successor, and whether Fanny will now go to live with Aunt Norris. Both are soon decided. Although Edmund is to be ordained, Tom's extravagance means that the living of Mansfield must be presented to an outsider, and Dr Grant is appointed. Fanny is upset at the prospect of leaving Mansfield, but Aunt Norris has no intention of looking after her. The Grants move into the Parsonage. A year passes. Sir Thomas and his eldest son leave for Antigua to deal with problems on a family estate.

Commentary

Tom's selfishness begins to cause problems for the rest of the family, and his inability to understand wrong behaviour is an alarming symptom, and indicates what is to come later in the novel. Mrs Norris displays another kind of selfishness in her attitude to Fanny, but notice how plausibly she manages to argue her case, although Jane Austen enables us to read between the lines.

Sir Thomas's departure marks the end of a kind of prelude in the structure of the novel. His absence removes a sense of authority from Mansfield, and although Sir Thomas is content to rely on Mrs Norris's vigilance and Edmund's judgement, both will prove inadequate.

Chapter 4

Sir Thomas is unable to return from Antigua, though Tom does. The old grey pony, which Fanny has learnt to ride, dies, and a replacement is found by Edmund, despite the opposition of Aunt Norris. Maria Bertram, encouraged by her aunt, is manœuvred into an engagement with Mr Rushworth, a neighbour. Mrs Grant has some visitors at the Parsonage – her half-brother and sister, Henry and Mary Crawford.

Commentary

Edmund's judgement is still sound, as we see when he manages to ensure that Fanny is provided with a replacement for the pony. Later on he will not be quite so anxious about her receiving regular exercise. Fanny's state of health is important throughout the novel, as well as the 'moral' health of everyone connected with Mansfield.

Maria's engagement is an important development, occurring as it does just before the arrival of the man who will destroy her marriage, and allows us to reflect on the character and conduct of all those directly involved. Lady Bertram can hardly be bothered to concern herself with it, although she is forced to visit Mrs Rushworth. Maria is concerned with Mr Rushworth's bank balance, and Mrs Norris's desire to be busy encourages Maria into accepting a man she does not love or respect. Edmund can see 'a fault in the business', but his sentiments are overruled by the others.

Mrs Grant, too, is planning a match for Mary Crawford, who has no objection provided she can 'marry well' and 'to advantage'. This is the first of several occasions when Jane Austen allows us to overhear the private conversations of the Crawfords.

Chapter 5

The Bertram girls are pleased to meet the Crawfords – particularly Henry, who is more than happy to flirt with both of them, despite Maria's engagement. Mary is attracted by Tom's position as eldest son into fancying that marriage with him would be a good proposition, and takes an interest in his sporting ventures. She is puzzled by Fanny's social position, but after a discussion with Tom and Edmund on the behaviour of young ladies decides that Fanny is not yet 'out'.

Commentary

Irony is found throughout the novel, but notice some telling examples in the opening paragraphs of this chapter. The Bertram girls 'were too handsome themselves to dislike any woman for being so too'. In other words they have a very high opinion of their own perfections, but their vanity is revealed by the simple phrase 'too handsome themselves'. Notice how Julia is 'quite ready to be fallen in love with' – a meaningful phrase if we take into account the discussion, later in the chapter, between Mary and Mrs Grant on the subject of what people expect from others in marriage.

The discussion on whether Fanny is 'out' or not helps us to see how an outsider views her. At this moment Fanny is very much the poor relation.

Chapter 6
While dining at Mansfield Mr Rushworth talks of improvements made to a friend's house, and of wanting to undertake similar ones at Sotherton. Fanny is concerned when she hears that an avenue might be cut down. Mary discusses the imminent arrival of her harp, and her feelings on both improvements and naval officers. Henry has made improvements on his own estate, and is readily persuaded to assist Mr Rushworth. At the instigation of Mrs Norris a visit to Sotherton is suggested as a party for all the young people, except Fanny.

Commentary
In a series of conversations over dinner, we are introduced to Mr Rushworth, and the theme of improvements as it relates to country houses.

Mary's comments on the harp show that her values are very different from those shared by Edmund and Fanny. She believes in 'the true London maxim, that everything is to be got with money', and finds difficulty in accepting that her personal desires are less important than 'getting in the grass'. Here, as elsewhere in the novel, we see the traditional country values in conflict with the fashionable ways of the town.

Chapter 7
Fanny and Edmund do not approve of Mary's comments on her uncle, but Edmund is attracted by Mary's beauty and lively personality. Mary, despite previous reservations, begins to admire him. With Edmund's encouragement she learns to ride, and makes increasing use of the mare Fanny rides. Expeditions are made by the young people to various parts of the neighbourhood. On four occasions Fanny is denied her daily ride and her health begins to suffer. Edmund returns from dining with the Grants to find Fanny in a state of exhaustion from running errands for her aunts, and is determined to ensure that she will receive adequate exercise in the future.

Commentary

During the course of this chapter Jane Austen makes us aware of Edmund's growing infatuation with Mary Crawford and his subsequent neglect of Fanny. The mare, which was obtained with Fanny in mind, is appropriated by Mary, and the events surrounding this action reveal some deliberate comparisons between the two women. Physical health is not the same as moral health, and while Mary does possess wit and charm, and makes a courageous horse-woman, she is also extremely selfish, unable to do what she knows to be right. Edmund indulges her selfishness, and Fanny's health suffers. Later on, his infatuation will help to worsen the moral health of the Bertram family. Fanny, despite her physical debility, is strong enough to struggle against 'discontent and envy'.

Chapter 8

Mr Rushworth and his mother visit Mansfield and the planned excursion to Sotherton is approved. Lady Bertram cannot be persuaded to go, but Mary Crawford is glad to accept. Maria and Julia are both anxious to share the driver's seat of the barouche with Henry. Despite protestations from Aunt Norris, Edmund decides to stay behind so that Fanny can go, but when Mrs Grant offers to act as Lady Bertram's companion, he changes his mind, and the Sotherton party is complete. Maria is upset when Julia sits next to Henry, but pleased to be acknowledged as the future mistress of Sotherton as they near their destination.

Commentary

The visit to Sotherton is one of the novel's important episodes, and is described in the next two chapters. Jane Austen manages to draw her characters together in interesting situations, and the relationships between them are explored with great subtlety. Sotherton is another large house, but it does not impose the same restrictions on the young people as Mansfield, and the garden setting helps to reinforce a sense of freedom.

Mrs Rushworth is one of those minor characters who might be overlooked in a first meeting, but who, nevertheless, gives depth to the novel's portrait of a social group, and plays a decisive role in the subsequent failure of Maria's marriage. Jane Austen cannot afford to spend too much time delineating her character, but manages to convey a great deal in a few words – 'a well-meaning, civil, prosing, pompous woman, who thought nothing of consequence, but as it related to her own and her son's concerns'.

Chapter 9

The party is welcomed by Mr Rushworth and his mother, and after lunch
is given a conducted tour of the house. In the chapel Fanny, Edmund and
Mary discuss the place of religion in the household, and Mary makes some
disparaging remarks about clergymen. Julia draws everybody's attention to
Mr Rushworth and Maria standing by the altar, while the latter receives
more flirtatious remarks from Henry. Julia reveals that Edmund is to be
ordained, and they all leave the chapel to gather eventually on the lawn.

Henry, Maria and Mr Rushworth are busy discussing improvements, so
Edmund, Fanny and Mary go for a walk in the wilderness, and the subject
of clergymen is continued – Mary doing her best to dissuade Edmund from
becoming one. They reach a bench by a locked gate. Edmund and Mary
cannot agree on the distance they have walked. Fanny is glad of an opportunity to rest while they continue their walk.

Commentary

Jane Austen employs a good deal of symbolism in this and the following
chapter. The various characters visiting the chapel reveal facets of their
moral outlook, especially Mary, who is completely taken aback by the
news that Edmund is to be ordained, and makes an unfortunate comment
on clergymen which causes the reader, as well as Fanny and Edmund, to
pause in surprise. Edmund and Fanny can see the value of family worship,
and the importance of the clergyman in instilling good principles, but
Mary ridicules both. The chapel, which might have restrained bad conduct
and maintained moral health, is no longer in use. Mary considers this an
improvement, like Mr Rushworth's plans for Sotherton in general, but
Edmund and Fanny cannot agree.

Chapter 10

Mr Rushworth, Maria and Henry Crawford arrive at the locked gate. Maria
wants to go into the park, and Mr Rushworth offers to fetch the key he
has forgotten to bring. While he is absent, Henry persuades Maria to slip
around the gate, despite Fanny's protests. Soon after their departure Julia
appears, angry at having been detained by Aunt Norris and Mrs Rushworth.
She, too, manages to get past the gate. Mr Rushworth returns with the
key. Fanny, after hearing his opinion of Henry, persuades him to follow
the others.

Fanny is concerned that Mary and Edmund have been gone so long,
and goes in search of them, only to discover that they have managed to

get into the park through another, unlocked gate. They have been sitting in the avenue which Fanny was hoping to see.

The visitors return to the house to dine, and eventually leave for home. Apart from Aunt Norris, who has been scrounging, they have all experienced a day of disappointments as well as pleasures.

Commentary

The conversation between Henry and Maria at the locked gate is full of double meanings. The gate itself seems to represent the conventional restraints imposed on Maria by her engagement to Mr Rushworth. Henry is anxious to assist her in finding a way round her problem, and the rehearsals for the play, as well as their walk in the park, will enable them to flirt with each other. This episode anticipates the subsequent elopement of the pair.

Chapter 11

Maria and Julia are not pleased with the news that Sir Thomas is to return in November, especially Maria, whose marriage will then take place. Mary Crawford shares their feelings, for she does not want Edmund to be ordained. During an evening spent at Mansfield she teases Edmund about his wish to become a clergyman, and ridicules the profession as a whole, despite arguments on the other side from Edmund and Fanny. The latter discuss the beauty of the scene outside, but Edmund's infatuation for Mary is becoming obvious, and Fanny watches him join her at the piano.

Commentary

This is a short chapter, which continues the 'ordination' debate with Mary's wit and vivacity matched against the more pedestrian sincerity of Edmund and Fanny. Are we tempted to agree with her or them? The example of Dr Grant might cause us to move towards Mary's position, but notice Edmund's argument – 'Where any one body of educated men, of whatever denomination, are condemned indiscriminately, there must be a deficiency of information, or . . . of something else.' It will take Edmund a long time to realise where Mary's deficiencies lie.

Meanwhile, Fanny finds herself the observer once more – alone by the window, contemplating both the noise and 'glee' of the 'busy' people by the piano, and the true 'harmony' of the 'natural' world. Jane Austen finds just the right words to suggest her heroine's 'enthusiasm' – a label she sometimes gives to characters of whom she does not approve – but they do not detract at all from the truth of what Fanny is saying.

Chapter 12

Tom returns from visiting friends, but Mary is now certain that she prefers Edmund. Henry spends two weeks on his estate, but finds that he misses the pleasure of flirting with the Bertram sisters who consider his absence equally tedious. Fanny is worried by the behaviour of Maria and Henry, but Edmund does not share her concern. He believes, like everyone else, that Henry is attracted to Julia.

At a hastily arranged dance Aunt Norris draws Mrs Rushworth's attention to the possibility of Julia marrying Henry Crawford, but Mrs Rushworth only has eyes for her son and his future bride. Fanny is disappointed when Tom cannot be bothered to dance with her, but amused when he subsequently asks her in order to avoid playing a game of whist.

Commentary

This chapter tells us more about the feelings of Henry, Maria and Julia, and the selfishness of Tom. The latter's gaffe in making a remark about Dr Grant, which he believes has been overheard, and his sudden desire to dance with Fanny are comic touches that help to establish Tom's character. He is by no means an unlikeable character - just thoughtless and inclined to view most things in a comical way.

The dance (Fanny's first!) reminds us just how enclosed the life of the country gentry, at that time, could be, but beneath the polite conversation and elegant manners lies the very real economic necessity of marriage. To women of Jane Austen's class it was the most crucial event in their lives, and dancing provided an opportunity to enjoy close contact with eligible men, while the financial aspects of marriage were debated at the side of the room by the chaperones.

Chapter 13

Tom's newly arrived friend, John Yates, fires all the young people with a desire to act. Edmund is concerned with the disruptions a play will cause, and believes that it would be improper considering Maria's situation. Sir Thomas would not approve. Despite these protestations from Edmund, silently supported by Fanny, Tom plans to turn the billiard room into a theatre. Maria and Julia will not give up the pleasure of acting, and Aunt Norris is only too pleased to be 'busy'. Edmund's opposition is further diminished when he hears that Mary is willing to take a part.

Commentary

The outsider - Mr Yates - initiates what is to become one of the novel's important episodes. Aside from the morality of acting, or the nature of the chosen play, we should take note of some of the words Jane Austen uses to illustrate the themes of change versus continuity, noise versus stillness, employment versus bustle, selfishness versus true feeling and honesty versus deceit or self-deceit. Thus we learn of Tom that he has 'so much leisure as to make almost any novelty a certain good', of Henry that 'in all the riot of his gratifications' acting 'was yet an untasted pleasure'. He longs 'to be doing something' and is quite capable of undertaking 'any character that ever was written'. Tom 'means nothing but a little amusement' while his sisters are 'quite as determined in the cause of pleasure'.

Key words such as 'novelty', 'pleasure', improvement', etc., are used throughout the novel, and we should be fully aware of their meaning and note their reoccurrence.

Chapter 14

The conversion of the billiard room is well under way, but no decision has been reached on the play to be performed. *Lovers' Vows* is chosen, but a disagreement arises between Maria and Julia because each wants to act opposite Henry Crawford. When he shows a preference for Maria, Julia walks off in a temper, and the other female lead is offered to Mary. Fanny reads the play herself and decides that it is a highly unsuitable choice.

Commentary

Fanny looks on in pity as selfishness is revealed in all the potential actors. Ostensibly they are choosing parts in a play, but Henry and the Bertram girls are in the process of acting out a little domestic drama of their own. So far, Henry has been content to flirt with both of them, but in selecting Maria as his Agatha he rouses Julia's jealousy, and encourages Maria's belief that he is genuinely in love with her. In 'assumed' characters they will now be given the opportunity to indulge their feelings openly. Henry's feelings are shallow, but Maria is genuinely stirred by his attentions.

Chapter 15

Mary Crawford agrees to play Amelia, and Mr Rushworth, Count Cassel. Edmund is unhappy at the choice of play and tries to persuade Maria that she ought not to act, but with no success. Maria is convinced that Julia would accept the part if she were to refuse it. Lady Bertram hasn't the energy to intervene, while Mrs Norris is only concerned with organising everybody and saving money. After dinner the Crawfords appear, and Mary asks who is to play Anhalt to her Amelia. The actors are concerned about this, and further discussions take place while Mary tries to persuade Edmund to take the part. Fanny is taken aback when Tom asks her to act, and despite her protests he tries to force her into compliance. Aunt Norris accuses Fanny of ingratitude, while Mary tries to comfort her. Tom comes to the conclusion that an outsider must be chosen to play Anhalt. Mary has her reservations.

Commentary

Lovers' Vows (the title is highly ironic) was translated from the German in the 1790s, and is a highly melodramatic piece, involving such indelicate matters as an illegitimate child and a forward young lady proposing marriage to a clergyman - the latter incident forming the scene between Edmund and Mary.

Jane Austen herself enjoyed amateur theatricals, and many readers cannot understand why acting should be condemned in this instance. Many possible answers appear in the text - Maria's situation, Sir Thomas's known opposition, the play itself - but we must also consider the moral aspect of acting, for many of Jane Austen's contemporaries felt that playing a part might encourage insincerity, and clearly she believes this to be the case with Henry.

Fanny, of course, cannot act - neither is she prepared to *play* a role in real life.

Chapter 16

Fanny is worried that she may still be asked to act, and goes to her room to consider the matter. Edmund appears, and asks for her advice. He feels that Tom's plan to bring in a stranger must be prevented, and has decided to act himself. Edmund wants Fanny's approval, but she withholds it, knowing that he is really swayed by his feelings for Mary. Alone, Fanny concludes that she was right in her decision not to act, but this is of less consequence now that Edmund has been persuaded into doing what he knows to be wrong.

Commentary

We learn a great deal about Fanny and her position in the family from the description of her room. She has found a niche for herself, but it lacks warmth, and becomes hers only because it is unwanted by others. It was the schoolroom, and Fanny continues to 'educate' herself by reading worthwhile books, even if the Bertram girls consider that the process of learning stops at sixteen. The objects in the room remind Fanny that she has found some affection at Mansfield, and they reflect her taste and character. 'Romantic' transparencies are highly suitable for a girl who admires nature and hoped for a melancholy chapel at Sotherton. Her beloved William is represented by a drawing of his ship, and the various work boxes are a sign that Fanny is always 'usefully' employed.

In solitude and stillness, away from the bustle of the drawing-room, Fanny finds time to debate the rightness of her actions, and is able to listen to the voice of her own conscience, which, as she later tells Henry Crawford, is our 'better guide'. Both the peace of the East room and Fanny's peace of mind are to be shaken by future events.

Chapter 17

Tom and Maria are pleased that Edmund has agreed to act. They believe that his *only* motive has been jealousy over Mary, who is even more delighted by his decision. Mrs Grant volunteers to act the part refused by Fanny. Julia is desperately unhappy at the treatment she has received from Henry. Mary and Mrs Grant discuss Henry's flirtations. Mary is aware that he prefers Maria, while Mrs Grant hopes he has no such designs on an engaged woman, and does not believe that Julia is feeling anything. In fact, Julia is longing for some disaster to overtake Maria. Edmund, Tom and Aunt Norris do not perceive what has happened - all three are too concerned with preparations for the play.

Commentary

An interesting chapter in which Jane Austen allows us time - just before events reach a climax - to reflect on the feelings of Fanny and Julia, both from inside the character, and, in Julia's case, through the eyes of others.

'She was full of jealousy and agitation.' It sounds like Julia, but, in fact, Fanny's feelings are being described. Despite her unhappiness, Fanny shows nothing of what she is enduring. She conquers her weakness, and pities Julia. Julia, on the other hand, sulks and makes unpleasant comments, and is too bothered about herself to realise that Maria is heading for trouble - neither is she the only guilty member of the family. Julia lacks not only 'affection', but 'principle'. In Chapter 9 we were told that her education had not included 'that higher species of self-command, that just consideration of others, that knowledge of her own heart, that *principle* (my italics) of right'. The same, alas, applies to Maria.

Chapter 18

Everything is now under way for the performance of *Lovers' Vows*, but Fanny, in whom almost everybody confides, begins to realise that all the actors are discontented. She enjoys watching Henry Crawford act, but is kept busy making costumes and helping Mr Rushworth learn his part. Fanny does not relish having to watch the love scene between Mary and Edmund, so she retires to her room. Here she is disturbed by Mary, who wants her assistance in preparing for the evening rehearsal. As they reach the half-way point in the scene, Edmund appears, and he and Mary rehearse together – much to the distress of Fanny who remains to prompt.

The first full rehearsal is about to start that evening, when the Crawfords arrive with the news that Mrs Grant must stay at home. Everyone turns to Fanny, who confesses to knowing the part, and she finally agrees to act. The rehearsal starts, but Julia rushes in with the news that Sir Thomas has returned.

Commentary

The return of Sir Thomas, which marked the end of the first volume in the original three-volume edition, is not only a superbly dramatic climax, but also symbolises the reassertion of authority in the lives of the would-be actors. Fanny is rescued by outside intervention just at the point of being obliged to participate in *Lovers' Vows*. In 'doing right' by the demands of her relations she has yielded on the question of acting. Temporarily, good nature gets the better of good judgement.

Chapter 19

All the actors are thrown into confusion. The Crawfords return to the Parsonage, while the Bertrams and Mr Rushworth troop off to the drawing-room. Fanny hesitates for a few moments, and then follows them, to be overwhelmed by Sir Thomas's greeting. The latter is very content to be with the family again as they settle round the fire to hear his news. The subject of the theatricals is narrowly avoided, but when Sir Thomas leaves in order to visit his bedroom, a hasty discussion quickly establishes that Mr Yates is alone in the theatre, and Tom goes after his father. Sir Thomas, disturbed by the alterations made to his room, walks through the billiard room door to find himself on stage with Mr Yates. Tom witnesses the encounter and introduces his friend.

They return to the drawing-room where all but Mr Yates perceive that Sir Thomas is far from pleased. No more acting will now take place.

Commentary

Fanny's meeting with Sir Thomas on his return is an important moment, and the minutes leading up to it are full of tension which eventually proves unfounded, for both are surprised by what they see. She sees him no longer as an ogre, but as a human being deserving and showing affection. He is impressed by her 'improvement in health and beauty'.

The actors all realise, almost instantly, the full implications of what they have been doing, especially when Sir Thomas is angered by the alterations in his room – yet another symptom of the 'infection' (Tom's choice of word) that has threatened the calm stability of life at Mansfield. Sir Thomas casts an eye over the billiard room to detect whether any material damage has been done to the house, but the serious damage remains, as yet, undetected, though it is clear to him that something improper has occurred.

During this chapter Yates provides a great deal of comic relief to the tension felt by others. His theatrical encounter with Sir Thomas is delightful, and so, too, is the subsequent conversation in the drawing-room, when, oblivious to the hints dropped by those around him, he persists in discussing the play. Yates's moral obtuseness and lack of propriety help to show up the failings of the Bertram children.

Chapter 20

Edmund apologises to his father for taking part in the play, and Sir Thomas sets about removing every trace of it from the house. He attempts to take Mrs Norris to task for allowing the young people to act, but without success – her only concern is Maria's marriage.

Sir Thomas is once again in control at Mansfield, and Mr Yates realises that the performance will not take place after all. Maria still hopes that Henry will declare his feelings for her openly, but his next visit proves to be his last, for he is on the point of leaving for Bath. Fanny is pleased to see the back of him, and, after the departure of Yates, Sir Thomas is satisfied that peace and tranquillity have been restored to his home.

Commentary

Lovers' Vows is at an end, and stability returns to Mansfield – or so Sir Thomas would like to believe, but in burning books, removing all material objects connected with the play, and sending Mr Yates packing, he has not managed to avert the troubles looming ahead. Because he is 'more willing to believe they felt their error, than to run the risk of investigation' and will 'not enter into any remonstrance with his other children', Sir Thomas is just sweeping the problem under the carpet. He is still totally unaware of the true feelings of his children, and his subsequent discussion with Maria (Chapter 21) confirms this. Sir Thomas fails also in his attempt to reprove Mrs Norris, not perceiving the threat she has always been to members of the family. Aunt Norris's judgement is generally at fault, and no more so than in her over-estimation of Mr Rushworth.

Lovers' Vows is over for Maria in a more obvious way. She must now face a loveless, mercenary marriage, while trying to hide all her feelings for Henry. They both resume their roles as polite inhabitants of the drawing-room, but while Henry is an adept at the game of pretence, Maria finds it a strain to maintain her composure.

Chapter 21

Edmund and Fanny discuss the change that has taken place since Sir Thomas's return. Fanny enjoys the peace and quiet, but Edmund misses the presence of the Crawfords. He also reveals that Sir Thomas has made some complimentary remarks about her. Fanny is concerned that Sir Thomas will not be so impressed with Mr Rushworth on further acquaintance, and this proves to be the case. Sir Thomas offers his support if Maria wishes to be released from her engagement, but, disappointed in her feelings for Henry Crawford, and longing to escape from restrictions at home, she declines it. Arrangements are made for the wedding, which occurs soon after.

Commentary

This is a transitional chapter which resolves some of the problems caused by the play, and hurries the reader on to Maria's marriage. We also begin, like Sir Thomas, to view Fanny in a new light – the ugly duckling is about to become the swan.

Maria's marriage is treated with heavy irony, for she has married for all the wrong reasons. We think back to the novel's opening paragraphs, for this is another marriage based on wealth and position rather than affection.

Chapter 22

Fanny finds herself in demand at the Parsonage now that her cousins have gone. Having initially invited Fanny in to shelter from the rain, Mary begins to discover that her visits provide welcome relief from the tedium of the country. Meetings occur regularly, and the two often walk in the Parsonage garden. On such an occasion they are joined by Mrs Grant and Edmund, who is glad to see that they are becoming such good friends. He is in love with Mary, but she still has reservations about marrying a poor country clergyman. Edmund and Fanny prepare to leave, but both are invited to dine at the Parsonage, and Edmund gives a conditional acceptance on Fanny's behalf.

Commentary

There is little that Fanny and Mary have in common, apart from their feelings for Edmund. Fanny enjoys the country, natural beauty and solitude, while Mary longs for the bustle of town life. Mary values Edmund the public man, while Fanny loves him for his kindness and warmth. For Mary, Fanny's visits are a 'novelty', while the latter cannot decide why she continues to call: 'it seemed a kind of fascination'.

Mary is equally puzzled by *her* increasing attachment to Edmund. She would normally find country life too quiet, but she has enjoyed the summer at Mansfield. A struggle is taking place inside this basically calculating young lady. Are her feelings for Edmund strong enough to overcome her wordly, if not mercenary, scruples? Would she be able to endure the frugal existence of a clergyman's wife, even if she could bring herself to marry one?

Chapter 23

Lady Bertram is surprised that Fanny should have been asked to dine with the Grants, but Sir Thomas gives his approval, and contingency plans are made for looking after Lady Bertram while Fanny is out. Aunt Norris does her best to ruin Fanny's enjoyment, but Sir Thomas shows great thoughtfulness towards her.

When she and Edmund arrive they discover that Henry has returned from Bath. This is not what Fanny had expected, and she finds him as morally reprehensible as ever in the way he discusses Maria and the theatricals. Edmund discusses his future as a clergyman with Dr Grant. Henry teases him about his first sermon, but Mary is upset by Edmund's persistent wish to be ordained.

Commentary

Within this chapter are two excellent examples of Jane Austen's ability to portray characters through the words they speak.

Aunt Norris sets out to pain and humiliate Fanny, and the phrases fall like a succession of hammer blows. Her first speech ('Upon my word Fanny. . .') reiterates the word 'you' twelve times in as many lines, and the pace at which this occurs leaves Fanny, the reader, and, at one point, Aunt Norris herself, almost breathless. The sharpness of the tone is highlighted by Fanny's meek reply, and Sir Thomas's equally gentle question about the carriage.

Henry, on the other hand, as an accomplished actor, is capable of endlessly modulating his tone to suit his listener. Notice how frequently

Jane Austen draws our attention to this as narrator: 'with a momentary seriousness', 'changing his tone again to one of gentle gallantry', 'breaking forth again', 'he continued, in a lower tone', 'in a calmer, graver tone, and as if the candid result of conviction'. These almost read like instructions in a play, and show the basic insincerity of Henry – particularly the words 'as if' in the last phrase. It is hardly surprising that later on Fanny cannot bring herself to accept seriously anything that Henry says. On the present occasion her own firm reply to him comes as a shock, and may, in part, account for the interest he shows in her. Henry has a winning tongue, but Fanny is not as easily deceived as her cousin.

Chapter 24

Henry announces to Mary that his visit will be prolonged in order to make Fanny fall in love with him. He dwells on Fanny's improved appearance, but Mary ascribes his motives to piqued vanity. Fanny is pleased by his politeness towards her. News arrives that William Price's ship has returned to England, and he soon appears at Mansfield, impressing everybody with his friendly, open character. Henry is moved by Fanny's affection for her brother, and begins to feel a genuine attraction for her, combined with envy of William, to whom he shows great kindness in lending a horse.

Commentary

Henry's plans to make a small hole in Fanny's heart initiate a new movement within the novel's structure, ending the lull which followed the *Lovers' Vows* episode. Their changing relationship now dominates the action until Fanny leaves for Portsmouth.

William is not only an important character in his own right, showing what self-discipline and principle can achieve given the right help, but he acts as a kind of catalyst between his sister and Henry. The latter realises that Fanny's heart is well worth winning, and can be reached through her brother, while Fanny is genuinely touched by Henry's kindness to William.

At the beginning of the chapter Henry confesses to being puzzled by Fanny's character. As readers, we do not share that difficulty, but from now on we *do* find ourselves continually surprised by facets of Henry's character that Jane Austen has kept hidden in order to tantalise us with the possibility of his moral reform.

Chapter 25

At a dinner engagement at the Parsonage Sir Thomas is pleased to observe Henry Crawford's attentions to Fanny. After dining, the party divides for games of whist and 'Speculation'. Henry reveals that by chance he has visited Thornton Lacey, which is to be Edmund's parish after his ordination. They discuss possible improvements to the house, but Edmund is adamantly against most of them – both he and Sir Thomas have strong views on the home and conduct of a parish priest.

William and Fanny discuss dancing, and the former voices a desire to see his sister dance. Henry praises Fanny's dancing, and continues the attentions he has been showing all evening by helping her on with her shawl.

Commentary

'Speculation' is a word generally used in connection with business enterprises involving the possibility of gain or loss. In the card-game, players buy and sell trump cards – the possessor of the highest being the winner. Jane Austen enjoyed the game, and mentions it several times in her letters, but within this chapter she uses it to symbolise a different kind of speculation – marriage. Earlier (Chapter 5) Mary had commented that marriage was a 'manœuvring business'. On this occasion she has been 'speculating' on the hope of marrying Edmund, but is disappointed when he repeats his intention of becoming a clergyman, for, to Mary, that would be a loss and not a gain – she would like to obtain a country gentleman with a fashionable residence. Mary hazards everything to win the card-game, as she will do later to win Edmund. Henry, naturally enough, is adept at the game, but as far as Fanny is concerned he must try to 'sharpen her avarice', in order to help her win. Fanny is not motivated by greed for a 'large income', and unlike her aunt and cousin would be happy to settle for a 'decent maintenance', but Sir Thomas, noticing Henry's behaviour, is about to indulge in a little 'speculation' on her behalf.

Chapter 26

Sir Thomas decides to give a ball at Mansfield for the benefit of Fanny and William. Even without the proffered help of Mrs Norris, the date is fixed, and invitations sent.

Edmund is delighted with the news, for Fanny's sake, but remains absorbed by the two issues facing him in the near future – ordination and the possibility of being married to Mary.

Not knowing what to wear for the ball, Fanny visits the Parsonage to consult Mary. They quickly decide on her clothes, but jewellery remains a problem, for Fanny has no chain to wear with a cross she has been given by William. Mary offers a chain from her own box – revealing afterwards that it was given to her by Henry. Fanny accepts the chain with some feelings of uneasiness.

Commentary
Edmund is concerned with choosing a profession and a wife; Fanny with choosing an item of jewellery, but Jane Austen wants us to see that all decisions, whether great or small, have a moral significance. The cross Fanny wears is symbolic, and shows her strong religious faith, as well as her affection for William. Edmund is later to provide a chain, when Mary's proves unsuitable – thus linking all the most important elements in Fanny's life.

Mary's chain, on the other hand, lives up to its name, for it weighs Fanny down with obligations she would rather not feel. Mary has become her friend by chance rather than conscious choice, and Fanny has a suspicion – well-founded as it turns out – that Henry is behind the present. Fanny is well aware that Henry's behaviour towards her has changed, and the necklace may be the first move in an attempt to entangle her as he had Maria.

Chapter 27
Fanny returns from the Parsonage to find Edmund in her room. He has brought her a chain for William's cross. Edmund is delighted to learn of Mary's gift, and will not allow Fanny to think of returning it. Fanny is deeply moved by this token of affection from her cousin.

Henry Crawford invites William to accompany him back to London in order to dine with the Admiral – an offer William cannot refuse, since it may increase his chances of promotion.

The preparations for the ball begin to agitate Fanny's nerves, and when she meets Edmund she is futher disturbed to learn that he has just returned from seeing Mary; Edmund has been to request the first two dances with Mary. He is upset by her attitude towards clergymen, but again reveals his affection for Fanny. On this slightly happier note, Fanny dresses for the ball.

Commentary
One of the fascinating features of Jane Austen's men and women is the very human way in which they display conflicting emotions. She is not a novelist who relies, in any way, on steroptyped characters - hers fluctuate rapidly from happiness to discontent as circumstances demand, and none more noticeably than Fanny in this chapter. By the time she is dressed for

the ball we probably feel as emotionally drained as she is. One moment of elation, like receiving Edmund's chain, is set against the pain of knowing how deeply he is attached to Mary, while news of Mary's dislike of clergymen again raises her spirits.

In the midst of all this emotional turmoil Fanny must try to maintain self-control, must not allow her feelings for Edmund to get the better of her judgement. Fanny must 'endeavour to be rational, and to deserve the right of judging Miss Crawford's character and the privilege of true solicitude for him (Edmund) by a sound intellect and an honest heart'. It is not always easy to subdue emotions, but Fanny acts on what she believes, in her conscience, to be right. In this lies her 'heroism of principle'.

Chapter 28
The ball at Mansfield takes place, and Fanny realises with a shock that this is her official 'coming out'; she must open the proceedings. Despite her shyness Fanny manages very well - dancing with both Henry and Edmund, who has been arguing with Mary. Henry's attentions to Fanny are noticed by Sir Thomas, who is pleased that the ball should have achieved what he had originally intended it should, and he invites Henry to take an early breakfast with William and Fanny. The latter, after a last glance around the room, retires to bed.

Commentary
The ball represents a considerable social triumph for the poor relation of the Bertrams. Fanny is launched into society as an attractive girl, with the additional advantages of being Sir Thomas's niece, and the object of Henry Crawford's attentions. She has managed, by opening the ball with Henry, to fill the position left vacant by her cousins. Sir Thomas has every right to feel proud of what Mansfield has done for her - there is no doubt that Fanny has 'improved' in appearance and manner, but he does not yet appreciate her real merits, and his approval must be placed alongside the more questionable satisfaction felt by Lady Bertram and Aunt Norris. Mansfield is highly successful in turning out elegant young ladies, but far from satisfactory in forming their minds.

If outwardly the evening is a success for Fanny, inwardly it proves a mixed blessing, and Jane Austen manages to convey in detail all the little doubts and anxieties felt by her heroine. Fanny is *supposed* to enjoy the evening because she is the centre of noise and attention and has managed to 'catch' Henry Crawford, but in fact she enjoys the evening *despite* these; her contentment arises from seeing William happy and from dancing 'soberly' with Edmund.

Chapter 29
William and Henry leave for London, and Edmund to stay with Mr Owen, a friend who is also preparing for ordination. The evening passes slowly at Mansfield without them, but the next day Fanny visits the Parsonage to discuss the ball. Sir Thomas and Lady Bertram are both glad that Fanny remains to support them in the absence of their own children.

Although Fanny settles down to a quiet life once more, Mary Crawford is more deeply disturbed by Edmund's absence. She still does not approve of his coming ordination, and now shows jealousy towards the sisters of Edmund's friend. Fanny refuses to be drawn on the subject, and will not confirm that Edmund is attracted to Mary.

Commentary
Another transitional chapter, bridging the time between the ball and Henry's return from London with unexpected plans. It provides Jane Austen with yet another opportunity to compare the characters of Fanny and Mary. The former is soon able to 'conform' to the quietness of life at Mansfield – for her, the everyday routine is sufficient. Used to solitude Fanny can quickly adjust to the absence of William and Edmund, whose purpose in leaving meets with her approval. She does not feel jealousy towards the Misses Owen or Mary herself, whose persistent questions about Edmund prove trying.

Mary, on the other hand, is ironically near the mark when she describes herself as a 'noisy evil' at Mansfield. She lacks any useful occupations, and without the company of others, proves to have few inner resources. Edmund's absence is a great misery, and she finds life in a country parsonage dull. Indeed, we are tempted to ask why she is so concerned about Edmund, when marrying him would result in a life-style she despises. Mary is torn by internal conflict – wanting the man, but unable to appreciate what he believes in and needs. She cannot see the real Edmund Bertram any more than she can see the Misses Owen, whose imagined characters are extensions of her own personality.

Chapter 30
Henry Crawford returns from London to declare, to an astonished Mary, that he intends to marry Fanny. Having recovered from the shock, Mary is delighted by the news, and they proceed to analyse Fanny's good qualities.

Henry is clearly attracted by her, and outlines all his plans for the future, although he will not reveal his motive in going to London. Maria and Julia will have to accept the situation. He will be able to do far more to ensure Fanny's happiness than Edmund and Sir Thomas have done.

Commentary
Surprise is important in the novel as a device for ensuring the continued interest of the reader. Some novels employ it badly, but a skilful writer uses surprise to reveal hidden aspects of character, or to suggest how fate operates in people's lives.

On this occasion we are as surprised by Henry's decision as Mary. We know him to be insincere – having already heard him planning to make Fanny fall in love with him – but, like Fanny, we have misinterpreted the evidence placed before us. All the little attentions he has shown her have not been a pretence, and he now speaks of Fanny with genuine admiration and fervour – even to the extent of praising those principles which he does not share with her. Henry, paradoxically, has himself been deceived into thinking Fanny's silence is a sign of her sharing his own feelings.

If we look back over the preceding chapters we can see how cleverly Jane Austen has provided clues to the change going on inside Henry, but we do only gather their full significance in retrospect. We must feel the surprise, but we must not view the change in Henry as in any way unlikely or arbitrary.

Chapter 31
Henry brings Fanny the news that, with Admiral Crawford's influence, William has been given promotion. Fanny is delighted, but even more astonished when Henry reveals his motive in wanting to help William – his love for her. She refuses to listen any more, and rushes out of the room.

Dinner that evening brings Henry to Mansfield yet again, bearing a note of congratulation from Mary. Fanny is uncertain what to think, but writes a hasty, confused note in reply. All the Bertrams are as pleased about William's success as Fanny, but the latter finds that her happiness is dampened by Henry's proposal.

Commentary
This chapter combines brilliantly a narrative of both the social behaviour of a small group of people, and the private thoughts of one of the group. The outward events of the day could be neatly plotted on a timetable: Henry's visit soon after breakfast, his interview with Fanny and Sir Thomas,

dinner, the conversation between Lady Bertram and Aunt Norris, Fanny writing the note, Henry's departure – of all these we are made clearly aware. The everyday life of the house continues, whatever surprising news is brought from outside. But beneath the social scene we are shown the struggle going on inside Fanny as she tries to find a satisfactory explanation for Henry's behaviour.

The conclusion of the original second volume leaves Fanny and the reader in uncertainty and suspense. We are conscious of the threat to her provided by Henry's wooing.

Chapter 32

Sir Thomas comes to the East room to inform Fanny that Henry has formally requested her hand in marriage. Fanny is upset by Henry's perseverance, but manages to convey to Sir Thomas her absolute refusal. Unable to reveal the truth about Henry, she is forced to sit and listen while Sir Thomas declares his approval of Henry as both man and suitor, and finally accuses her of ingratitude. Fanny breaks down, and Sir Thomas leaves her alone for a few minutes. He returns to say that Henry has now left, but has requested an interview with Fanny. He wishes the whole affair to be kept from her aunts, and gives Fanny an opportunity of regaining her composure. Sir Thomas orders a fire to be lit in the East room; the first occasion on which this has happened since the room became Fanny's.

At dinner that evening Fanny is reprimanded yet again by Aunt Norris, and later she is requested to attend Sir Thomas in his room. On entering she is confronted by Henry Crawford.

Commentary

The scene between Fanny and Sir Thomas is a highly dramatic one, and much of it is rendered in direct rather than reported speech. The silences are filled with explanations of what the characters are thinking and feeling, while detailed notes of their movements enable us to visualise the scene in a vivid manner.

We sympathise completely with Fanny over the question of not wanting to marry without affection, but we can also understand Sir Thomas's exasperation, particularly since Fanny is unable to reveal the whole truth about Henry Crawford. We cannot admire Sir Thomas for wanting to force Fanny into a socially acceptable marriage – we remember his earlier dealings with Maria – but on the other hand we do appreciate the general tolerance and consideration he continues to display towards Fanny. The missing ingredient, of course, is affection, and for the lack of that we do condemn him. Fanny *does* want to 'go her own way', but not through wilfulness, as in Maria's case, but because she is listening to the demands of her conscience.

Heroines forced into marriages by domineering parents or guardians were common in eighteenth-century fiction and drama, but Jane Austen's version is more subtle than most. It does not rely on stereotyped characters for its success. Sir Thomas is not a greedy, scheming parent, and our awareness of his good qualities adds both tension and a sense of realism to the encounter.

Chapter 33

Henry is not prepared to give up too easily his wooing of Fanny, and he continues to declare his love for her without any success, since Fanny has no intention of marrying him. At first her replies are gentle, because of Henry's kindness to William, but gradually his persistence becomes intolerable.

Sir Thomas is disappointed by Henry's failure, but assures him that he may continue to visit Mansfield in order to change Fanny's opinion. To Fanny he behaves with forbearance, but is forced to relate Henry's proposal to her aunts. Aunt Norris is grimly silent, but Lady Bertram is disappointed that her niece has not accepted a man with such an income.

Commentary

Lady Bertram's advice is to be taken ironically of course, since she voices a wordly and mercenary view of marriage. The threat to Fanny's happiness and peace of mind is not diminished by our sense of Lady Bertram's shortcomings, indeed her indolence has allowed Maria to enter into a 'doomed' relationship because it fulfils all society's notions of a good marriage.

Chapter 34

Edmund returns to Mansfield and hears of Henry's proposal from Sir Thomas. He believes that Fanny ought to accept and that it is only a matter of time and gentle persuasion before she does.

Henry is invited to dine, and after dinner, when he and Edmund have joined the ladies, proceeds to read a scene from Shakespeare. Fanny is clearly moved by his talent for portraying the various characters, and Edmund begins to hope that she will be won over. The young men discuss preaching, and a chance remark of Henry's receives a sign of disapproval from Fanny. Henry renews his attempts to break down her resistance, once again affirming his love and constancy. Only the arrival of tea affords Fanny any relief from him.

Commentary

Henry's ability to impersonate various characters in reading aloud reminds us of his acting in *Lovers' Vows*, but it also highlights another matter Jane Austen is exploring – sincerity. In this chapter, for the first time, he admits to one of his own failings, and Fanny is quick to spot it. Up till now he has been content to play a series of roles without ever facing up to his own nature or listening to his own conscience. He *would* be able to speak the words of a church service better than Edmund, but his statements would be meaningless in the end, because they would not be sincerely held. Fanny cannot believe his declarations of love because she does not feel that his heart is in them, after all he has already exchanged false 'lovers' vows' with Maria.

However, Henry's 'insincerity' is given every outward advantage. We are intended to admire his witty conversation, and his eloquence does entertain us as much as his taste in reading effects Fanny. The question is really whether these abilities are used for a genuine moral purpose or merely to display the ability of the man himself. Great talents require careful supervision, and in *Mansfield Park* it is better to be silent and sincere than eloquent and hollow.

Chapter 35

Edmund, with his father's encouragement, has a long talk to Fanny. He applauds all her actions so far, but ventures the hope that Henry's perseverance will eventually be rewarded. Fanny tries to make him understand why she disapproves of Henry, but without success, for Edmund is once again under the influence of Mary Crawford and will not see Henry's faults for what they really are. Edmund reveals that the present situation is openly discussed at the Parsonage. Mary has been upset by Fanny's refusal, and wishes to have an interview with her before leaving Mansfield.

Commentary

Beneath what Fanny and Edmund appear to be saying runs a deeper note – her unspoken love for him, and his own infatuation for Mary – and neither can finally admit the whole truth to the other. Edmund, who is still trying to convince himself that Mary would make a good wife, undertakes a similar task in respect of Fanny and Henry. He is equally deceived by brother and sister. Fanny, on the other hand, is disturbed by the thought that her behaviour may appear irrational because social conventions prevent her declaring to Edmund that it is her love for him that stands in Henry's way. Her general analysis of the ways a woman ought to respond to a man's declarations is the only way she can illustrate her dilemma. A young lady of Jane Austen's era was expected to remain silent until approached by a young man - only then was she given official sanction to indulge her own feelings on the matter. It is the knowledge of what cannot be spoken between her and Edmund that oppresses Fanny.

Chapter 36

Mary Crawford arrives to talk to Fanny, but once in the East room, her recollection of the rehearsal with Edmund is stirred, and she reminisces about the week of acting. She is sorry to be leaving Mansfield and does not appear to feel much affection for the 'friends' she is going to visit, recounting their disastrous marriages for Fanny's benefit. Fanny's conquest of Henry is hailed as a triumph, and, in passing, Mary reveals that the necklace had been intended as Henry's gift from the outset. The two ladies discuss his flirtatious habits - Mary contemplating a future life for Henry and Fanny at Everingham. The latter's emotions are troubled by another reference to William's promotion and the imminent departure of Mary. Fanny promises to write. After another evening visit, Henry leaves with his sister for London.

Commentary

Henry's declaration is a climax in the novel's structure and is followed by a series of conversations which reveal the feelings of all those directly involved. The events have covered about twelve days from the time of the proposal to the Crawford's departure, but the intensity of the emotions felt by Fanny disguises the actual time involved.

London only appears in the novel by allusion, but Mary's remarks about her fashionable friends should alert us to the values it represents in opposition to Mansfield. Friendship appears to be based on habit rather than affection, marriage a question of convenience rather than love and even Mary - herself a product of the city - admits that Mansfield has 'heart'. It is ironic that Mary should be trying to push Fanny into one of the relationships she claims to deplore - 'She could not do otherwise than accept him, for he was rich, and she had nothing.' The Crawfords have both felt real affection at Mansfield, but old London habits will prove too strong in the end.

Chapter 37

Sir Thomas is surprised that Fanny has not shown any regret at the departure of Henry Crawford, but puts it down to the arrival of William Price on a visit. Edmund is equally astonished to find that Fanny does not miss Mary. Both father and son agree that a visit to her parents at Portsmouth would be good for Fanny. Sir Thomas hopes that an absence from wealth and elegance might incline her to accept Henry's offer.

Fanny is delighted to be going home after so many years and looks forward to being surrounded by an affectionate family once more. Lady Bertram is persuaded into managing without Fanny. Aunt Norris contemplates paying a visit to her sister – to the horror of William and Fanny – but she finally decides against the idea for financial reasons. Brother and sister leave Mansfield, and Fanny is saddened at having to say goodbye to the house and its occupants.

Commentary

A great deal of necessary information is given in this chapter which rounds off a section of the novel. Jane Austen's primary concern is to get Fanny to Portsmouth and away from Mansfield without too much delay. The change in environment is the crucial issue, but, even so, there is time for ensuring that the reader has grasped certain salient points. We must be fully aware of Sir Thomas's purpose in sending Fanny away. His little experiment does produce the result he had hoped for; Fanny is exiled from the way of life she has come to need. She does miss Mansfield and its occupants, and begins to view Henry in a new light.

We must also be aware that Fanny has high expectations of her family and their home life. Without her ideals we will not appreciate fully the irony when Fanny is faced with the realities of life at Portsmouth.

Finally we must believe, like Fanny, that Edmund's engagement to Mary is only a matter of time. Like her, we anticipate the arrival of the letter that will confirm all her worst fears. That threat remains in the back of our minds through the subsequent chapters.

Fanny's departure from the house is as emotional a scene as her arrival eight years earlier, but the rooms and their occupants that were so forbidding to the child have become dear and familiar to the young woman.

Chapter 38

After a journey of two days Fanny and William arrive at Portsmouth. They are greeted, by various members of the family, with the news that William's ship has left the harbour prior to sailing. Fanny is surprised by the smallness of the house, but pleased to see her mother, her brother Sam, and her sisters Susan and Betsey. Mrs Price orders tea to be prepared, and soon afterwards Mr Price enters. He greets William affectionately, but seems to have little time for Fanny, who is shocked by his manner and language. Tea still does not appear, and more noise is caused by the return from school of Tom and Charles, who romp around the house. Mrs Price goes off to supervise the fitting of William's uniform and Fanny is left alone with her uncommunicative father to contemplate the noise and confusion of the household. Eventually tea arrives. William appears in his uniform, but only a few minutes later he leaves in the company of a fellow officer.

The ladies are left alone, but Mrs Price appears to be uninterested in hearing about Mansfield, and soon the conversation is brought to an end by a violent quarrel between Susan and Betsey about a silver knife - once the property of another sister, now dead. Again Fanny is shocked by the behaviour and sentiments of her mother and sisters, and retires to bed early.

Commentary

This is a long and eventful chapter in which Jane Austen's readers must absorb a great deal of information. New characters appear accompanied by much news about naval matters, and in no time the reader is as stunned as Fanny herself. In Portsmouth there is no time for formal introductions, instead we are given lightning sketches of Mrs Price and the children, while Mr Price is presented in all the immediacy of his own language.

In these Portsmouth chapters Jane Austen attempts to depict a kind of home life that is not shown in any of the other novels, and it is done with a kind of comic realism that anticipates some of Charles Dickens's middle-class interiors. Portsmouth is as believable as Mansfield Park. The inhabitants of this Portsmouth house speak and behave like real human beings and it is filled with the kind of everyday objects that surround us where-ever we live - Fanny's band-box, Mr Price's newspaper and candle, the hastily washed tea-cup, the shirt sleeve and the silver knife.

Chapter 39

A week passes and Fanny begins to despair of her parents' home. William has sailed, and in his absence Fanny feels more isolated than ever. Her father is coarse, her mother a 'slattern', Betsey and the younger boys uncontrollable, and Susan possesses a very uncertain temper. Sir Thomas's plan seems to be working, for Fanny sadly misses Mansfield and its orderly ways.

Commentary

A short chapter this, covering more actual time than the previous one, but
being analytical rather than narrating events. It is constructed as a series of
contrasts which are central to the main themes of the novel – order versus
disorder, noise versus stillness, harmony versus contention, good management versus bad management and propriety versus impropriety. Mrs Price
is compared to her sisters, and we recall the opening chapter's description
of their marriages.

But we should not allow this deliberate contrast to influence our
judgements too greatly at this stage. After all, Fanny has not yet found
herself a 'niche' – apart from helping with Sam's wardrobe – and while
Portsmouth does not possess many obvious merits Fanny is soon to be
made painfully aware of Mansfield's deficiencies.

Chapter 40

Fanny is pleased to receive a letter from Mary Crawford telling her about
Maria's social progress in London, as well as the whereabouts of Edmund
and Henry. She finds no congenial company in Portsmouth, but gradually
comes to perceive good qualities in her sister Susan, settling one cause of
continuing irritation by buying Betsey a silver knife of her own. Susan
and Fanny begin to spend more time together reading and sewing.

Commentary

The silver knife is another of the important objects in the novel, tokening
a small but significant act of initiative on Fanny's part. She has been
taught and improved at Mansfield, but that is not enough. Even if she
cannot contemplate reforming Henry through marriage, she can be responsible for her younger sister. Fanny has been used to receiving presents (all
those netting boxes from Tom, Edmund's chain); now she must learn to be
a donor. Edmund has guided her taste in reading; she passes her knowledge
on to Susan. At Mansfield she has accepted her subservient role; at
Portsmouth she must face up to responsibilities. Susan's need prompts
her, and Susan's failure shows what ought to be done. Susan could do with
some of Mansfield's orderly ways, but Mansfield itself needs the affection
and strength of Portsmouth, which Fanny begins to recognise in Susan's
character.

Chapter 41

Fanny, still awaiting news of Edmund, is surprised by the sudden arrival
in Portsmouth of Henry Crawford, and even more astonished by his polite

behaviour towards her parents – especially her father whom they encounter on a walk. Henry has much to say of the business he has been undertaking on his Norfolk estate and confirms that Edmund is now in London. He anticipates a delightful summer and autumn at Mansfield, when two possible marriages have taken place. Mr Price asks Henry to dine with them that evening, but Fanny is most grateful when he is unable to accept.

Commentary

Another chapter of improvements! Henry is endeavouring to fulfil what he had promised at Mansfield – he will show his devotion to Fanny through his conduct. He is polite to Mr Price, with no signs of disdain or disapproval, and to Mrs Price he shows 'a degree of friendliness' as well. To Fanny he behaves with great tact, anticipating all her anxieties, and rarely causing her embarrassment. She begins 'to feel the possibility of his turning out well at last'.

The most important change in Henry, however, is the interest he is now taking in the welfare of the tenants on his estate for whom he is responsible. To a certain extent, of course, he is still playing a role, but at least it is a worth-while one – comprehending 'real business' and a sense of 'performing a duty', which so far in his life he has usually avoided. 'Here he had been acting as he ought to do.' The Henry Crawford who shows interest in the poor even sounds more serious, due to the extremely clever device Jane Austen employs of switching from direct to reported speech. This helps to focus our attention on the implications for Fanny of what Henry is saying.

Chapter 42

Henry accompanies the Price family to church, and afterwards for a walk on the ramparts. It is a fine day, but he is concerned with Fanny's lack of exercise, suspecting that her health is deteriorating. Aware of Fanny's situation at Mansfield, and fearing that she may be neglected, Henry offers to come and take her back whenever she is ready. He debates whether to return to Norfolk to supervise his estate. Fanny, having been escorted to the front door by Henry, continues to be much impressed by his improvement, but hopes that his new-found sensitivity will prevent him from pressing her with his attentions in the future.

Commentary

Many readers find Fanny's tendency towards ill health irritating, especially when combined with her moral goodness, and, indeed, compared with some of Jane Austen's other heroines, Fanny can appear to lack vitality, but again this is part of the overall design of her character. Christian heroines in literature are often depicted as weak and ailing. It is as if their spiritual goodness, their very *un*-worldliness can shine through all the more strongly. To Henry, Fanny appears an 'angel', and her advice to him on the importance of conscience in all personal matters certainly appears other-worldly, when we consider how much our lives are ruled by compromise.

Fanny's ill health is also a comment on the kind of environment she requires in order to live a good life – both physically and morally. The Price family appears to advantage on Sundays (the influence, however ironically, of regular religious observance), but Mrs Price's appearance has suffered from all the years of hardship she has undergone. William and Susan possess strong constitutions, but Fanny needs those gifts that Mansfield alone can provide – fresh air, regular exercise – a kind of existence in which the individual is in harmony with the natural world. Fanny sees Nature as a source of health and wisdom, and in so doing comes closer than all Jane Austen's other heroines – with the possible exception of Anne Elliot in *Persuasion* – to sharing the beliefs of Romantic writers like William Wordsworth and Samuel Taylor Coleridge.

Chapter 43

Fanny receives a letter from Mary containing information about what has been happening in London. Henry has returned from Portsmouth, while Edmund has arrived, and been admired by Mary's fashionable friends. The offer of conveying Fanny back to Mansfield is repeated, and the letter ends with a comment about Henry's return to Norfolk being delayed – he is required at a party of Mary's which Maria will also be attending.

Fanny's response to the letter is mixed. Edmund has not yet proposed to Mary, but this event will probably occur soon. She hopes that Henry will return to Norfolk rather than face Maria Rushworth.

Susan's improvement takes up more of Fanny's time, and the latter begins to feel sorry at the future prospect of leaving her at Portsmouth when Mansfield could do her so much good.

Commentary

Many eighteenth-century novels, including some of Jane Austen's earlier attempts at fiction, were written in the form of a series of letters exchanged by a small group of characters. It was a method that presented events from a series of viewpoints, and allowed for a deep analysis of individual thoughts and feelings, but it was not a flexible enough medium for Jane Austen's mature fiction, and only odd traces survive here and there. In this chapter, for example, without the voice of the narrator, it would have been necessary for Fanny to write to a third person about *her* reaction on reading Mary's letter, and Susan's educational progress.

In these chapters Jane Austen's use of letters serves a variety of purposes, which deserves a much closer analysis than can be given here. They provide a great deal of information in a short space, keeping Fanny in touch with the outside world while effectively reminding us of her isolation – a visit to London at this stage would be an unnecessary digression. Like Fanny we are kept in suspense at the likely outcome of events, and Jane Austen can spring her surprises to great effect without in any way deceiving us. Letters also serve to enlarge the number of fictional voices we hear at a time when Fanny's circle of acquaintance is particularly narrow. Jane Austen had learnt from Samuel Richardson, one of her favourite novelists, how much of a character can be conveyed by letter-writing.

Chapter 44

Fanny receives a letter from Edmund giving particulars of his visit to London. He has met Mary at the house of her friend, but, upset by her altered behaviour, has not yet proposed to her. This he intends to do by letter, now that he is back at Mansfield. Henry and Maria have met at a party, and the latter has shown indifference. She is living in a grand style, with Julia still as a companion, and appears to be happy with Mr Rushworth. Mansfield is missing the presence of Fanny.

Fanny is angered by Edmund's continuing infatuation, but pleased in contemplating his feelings for her.

Lady Bertram writes to inform Fanny that Tom has been taken ill. Edmund has gone to nurse him and bring him home. This is followed by another letter in which, after seeing the true state of her son's health, Lady Bertram expresses genuine concern. At Portsmouth Tom's health is of interest only to Fanny and Susan.

Commentary

Another of this novel's concerns is the contrast between what characters appear to feel, and what they actually feel. In the fashionable London society we hear about, friendship counts for little, and marriage is a matter of economics rather than love. Even between Lady Bertram and her sister, Mrs Price, the ties of blood are not strong enough to last many years of separation. The genuine emotions Mary Crawford and her brother experienced at Mansfield are swamped by the artificial manners of Mrs Fraser's circle. Tom Bertram's 'friends' leave him alone in his sickness, and only Edmund's ministrations restore him to health. Fanny is never entirely convinced of the Crawfords' feelings for her, and is herself unhappy at having her own misinterpreted by others. Edmund cannot yet perceive Fanny's feelings towards him.

On the other hand, we *are* shown the warmth of affection felt by those characters upon whom the future of Mansfield will rest - Fanny and Edmund, William and Susan, Edmund and his brother, and eventually Fanny and Sir Thomas, who finally realises how much she is needed at Mansfield. Even Lady Bertram, whose feelings have remained dormant for much of the novel, shows maternal concern for Tom. Fanny's search for love, which began with Edmund's kindness at Mansfield, and brought her to Portsmouth, will lead her back to the place and people she loves the most.

Chapter 45

Fanny continues to receive news of Tom's state of health, which is far more serious than Lady Bertram has led herself to believe. Edmund, fully occupied in nursing his brother, has not yet written to Mary.

The coming of spring serves to remind Fanny how long she has been away from Mansfield, and she is concerned that, as yet, no plans have been made to return her to the place where she can be of so much use to others.

Further proof of Mary's heartlessness is provided in a letter, ostensibly requesting information about Tom's health, but revealing how eager the writer is to see Edmund become the eldest son. Mary also reveals that Henry is continuing to see Maria, in the absence of her husband. Fanny is shocked by the letter's contents, and will not even contemplate the renewed offer of the Crawfords to convey her back to Mansfield - Sir Thomas would not approve. It now seems more than likely that, in the event of Tom's death, Mary will agree to marry Edmund, even though he is a clergyman.

Commentary

Jane Austen does not give long and detailed descriptions of the country-side, and yet in all her mature novels we are made aware of the influence it has on her fictional characters, particularly Fanny who possesses a Romantic appreciation of natural surroundings. In the natural world Fanny has found peace, harmony, beauty and a source of true wisdom in contemplating the works of a divine creator.

It is interesting to reflect here, as elsewhere in the novel, on Jane Austen's use of the word 'liberty'. To the Crawfords it means 'license', or being allowed to act as they please without any restraint. For them, 'liberty' is to be found in saying whatever suits them at the time, and indulging their own selfish inclinations. To Fanny, 'liberty' is to be found in the peace and solitude of the park, where contemplation leads to understanding. She has to face up to autocratic authority far more than any other young person in the novel, supported by her conviction that the individual conscience is the finest guide we all possess.

Chapter 46

Fanny receives a puzzling letter from Mary which seems to connect Henry with some kind of scandalous event at Wimpole Street, the Rushworths' London home. The next day brings no further news, but some gossip in Mr Price's newspaper suggests that Maria has run off with Henry. Fanny is deeply shocked, but further reflection convinces her that it is only too likely, and she feels pity for all those directly concerned. A letter from Edmund confirms the news, adding that Julia has eloped with Mr Yates. Fanny is requested to return to Mansfield, bringing Susan with her. Edmund arrives early the next morning, and is deeply moved at seeing Fanny again, although he says little on the subsequent journey. Fanny is delighted to see Mansfield Park, and is warmly greeted by Lady Bertram.

Commentary

The diversity of styles used in this chapter is remarkable, and shows how quickly Jane Austen can move from one method of narration to another. The fairly neutral tones of the opening are soon followed by Mary's letter, full of agitation, but nevertheless a good example of Mary's speaking voice. Fanny's reaction is told in such a way that, despite the presence of the narrator, we feel close to Fanny's own thoughts.

Jane Austen's description of sunlight in the Prices' parlour is very detailed and naturalistic, while the following paragraphs contrast the coarse, vulgar speech of Mr Price with the flowery prose of the newspaper's gossip column. Further diversity is provided by the clipped, but dignified style of Edmund's letter, echoed, briefly, in his remarks to Fanny.

Chapter 47

Fanny and Edmund help to console Tom and Lady Bertram, but Aunt Norris is overwhelmed by the news of Maria's disgrace, and can find little time for being unpleasant to Fanny and Susan. Lady Bertram gives Fanny all the details of the elopement – Maria and Henry have not been found, and Mrs Rushworth has managed to advertise the scandal. Fanny pities Sir Thomas. All his children are causing him grief in some way – even Edmund.

Three days after her return Fanny receives from Edmund an account of his last meeting with Mary. He has been shocked by her reaction to the scandal, for she believes that Maria's reputation might be salvaged by an eventual marriage with Henry. She has spoken lightly of Maria's disgrace, and shown displeasure that Fanny did not 'fix' Henry's inclinations by marrying him. Edmund has finally seen Mary's true nature – her lack of principle – and made her aware how much she has hurt him. Mary had joked about his moral views, and flirted with him, but all in vain. Edmund now regrets having left so abruptly, for he will never find another woman like her.

Commentary

Edmund's final interview with Mary is a crucial and revealing encounter calling for careful reading. It highlights the central moral issues of the novel, and opens the way to marriage for Edmund and Fanny, whose views on characters and events now coincide. Edmund's awakening, and his father's subsequent increased self-awareness, finally justify Fanny's moral stance with regard to the Crawfords. Like her brother, Mary has been given the chance to 'improve', but his vice and her folly have ruined their chances of happiness. Edmund's analysis of Mary's faults is accurate. Her greatest fault is 'ignorance'. She has not been taught to believe in any principles, and as a result is too easily governed by the attitudes and habits of others. We might also add that never before has Mary known much affliction, and, like Henry, she is lacking in self-knowledge.

Mary's last attempt to win back Edmund is significant. Her smile is described as 'saucy' and 'playful'. It is intended to be seductive, but this time Edmund realises what she is doing. Mary is revealed as the traditional temptress – manipulating men by employing her personal charms, and traditional, since female characters like her occur in many works of literature. Jane Austen's earlier novel *Lady Susan* had explored just such a heroine who is charming, but morally corrupt.

Chapter 48

Fanny's happiness is complete now that Edmund has seen through Mary Crawford. Sir Thomas blames himself for approving Maria's marriage – he has not fully understood the hearts of his children, and their education has not taught them any moral principles. Maria's disgrace is complete, but Sir Thomas can find comfort in the improvement of his remaining children.

Mr Rushworth obtains a divorce. Maria, finally realising that Henry will never marry her, settles away from Mansfield with Aunt Norris, whose departure is welcomed by Sir Thomas. Henry Crawford, who as a man does not share Maria's social disgrace, must continue to regret that his own selfishness has deprived him of Fanny. The Grants leave Mansfield for London where Dr Grant has been made a deacon. On his death, Mary continues to live with her half-sister, regretting that none of the eligible young men can quite rival Edmund.

Edmund finally begins to realise that he has loved Fanny all along. With the approval of Sir Thomas they are eventually married. The Price family continue to repay Sir Thomas's kindness, and Susan takes Fanny's place at Mansfield. On the death of Dr Grant, Edmund and Fanny move into the Parsonage.

Commentary

Jane Austen steps forward in her role of narrator to bring the story to its conclusion. By referring to her heroine as 'my Fanny', and allowing the reader to decide when Edmund realises his true feelings towards Fanny, Jane Austen achieves the effect of distancing herself, and the reader, from her fictional characters.

Many readers find the ending unsatisfactory. They feel that the elopement has been too deliberately contrived in order to ensure a traditional happy ending. On the other hand, we know enough about the relationship that existed between Henry and Maria to believe that such an outcome was possible if not probable. A reader must judge for himself, in the final analysis, whether the ending is natural or contrived.

Virtue is rewarded, folly reproved and vice punished, at least as far as the author is concerned, although in a rare example of the intrusion of her own religious beliefs, Jane Austen reminds us that we may receive 'a juster appointment hereafter', like Henry Crawford. The novel began with an act of patronage on Sir Thomas's part, and it concludes with an affirmation of the strength of the house in the lives of all those connected with it.

3 WHAT THE NOVEL IS ABOUT

3.1 MORAL ISSUES

Through the behaviour of her central characters, Jane Austen examines certain moral issues of universal significance. Like most eighteenth-century writers she believed that fiction should teach as well as entertain, and in *Mansfield Park* we are more aware of this than in any of her other novels. After the publication of *Pride and Prejudice* she commented, in a letter, that it was 'rather too light and bright, and sparkling', and though this playful remark rather ignores the moral content of that novel, it certainly could not be applied to *Mansfield Park*. On the contrary, many readers feel that the later novel lacks wit and vivacity – that it is rather solemn and preaches too obviously at them. Those readers who admire Elizabeth Bennet complain that Fanny Price is insipid, and that the Crawfords, who share Elizabeth's fondness for 'follies and nonsense, whims and inconsistencies', are treated unfairly, if not vindictively, by their creator. In doing this, though, they miss the whole point Jane Austen wishes to make, for though the Crawfords *are* entertaining characters, and undoubtedly possess all the social graces, their morals are lax in a way that Elizabeth Bennet's never were – they are 'unprincipled', and the word 'principles' is used many times in the novel to emphasise its author's moral concerns.

Jane Austen's moral principles were those of her class and upbringing. She believed in the Christian virtues, and Fanny Price embodies many of them – gentleness, humility, patience, courage, loving-kindness. Fanny doesn't always find it easy to act in the ways these would direct her – for example, she must overcome a great deal of natural timidity in order to stand up to Sir Thomas, and Edmund's infatuation for Mary Crawford sorely tries her patience – but eventually the Christian virtues do triumph over guile and deception. In fact, they nearly manage to make a convert out of Henry Crawford. We might even choose to think of *Mansfield Park* as a kind of moral fable or allegory, indeed, the episode of the locked gate in the grounds of Sotherton could have been taken from a work like *The Pilgrim's Progress* in order to demonstrate the dangers inherent in not observing moral restraints. Jane Austen believed that certain standards of behaviour were a necessity in civilised society. Even her own loathing of some aspects of the society around her was expressed indirectly through comic irony, and she would have been horrified with a world that exalted *rights* rather than *duties*.

Towards the end of the novel there is an interesting conversation between Fanny and Henry. The latter asks for advice, and the dialogue continues:

> 'I advise! – you know very well what is right.'
> 'Yes. When you give me your opinion I always know what is right. Your judgment is my rule of right.'
> 'Oh no! – do not say so. We have all a better guide in ourselves if we would attend to it, than any other person can be.'   (Chapter 42)

Here Jane Austen, through Fanny, asserts the importance of the individual conscience in determining what is right or wrong. Henry has never allowed his actions to be influenced by moral restraints, and in the course of the novel we see him trifling with the feelings of Julia and Maria Bertram. Like his sister he has been brought up in a household where morality has not been encouraged (the narrator describes Admiral Crawford as 'a man of vicious conduct') and the merely outward forms of Christianity, like regular church attendance, have had no effect. On the occasion quoted above, Henry's lack of any moral conscience is crucial, since he is debating whether to return to his estate or to London where he will encounter Maria, now married to Mr Rushworth. He cannot decide for himself, cannot do what *ought* to be done, and Fanny refuses to be his conscience. Henry returns to London, and subsequently elopes with Maria – 'Had he done as he intended, and as he knew he ought, by going down to Everingham after his return from Portsmouth, he might have been deciding his own happy destiny. But . . . the temptation of immediate pleasure was too strong for a mind unused to make any sacrifice to right.' Jane Austen believes that we all have a sense of right and wrong which can either be nurtured or destroyed by our upbringing and education.

Fanny Price, who might very well have been made envious or mercenary by her upbringing, has managed to maintain those principles which Edmund recognises on her first arrival at Mansfield Park: 'He . . . was convinced of her having an affectionate heart, and a strong desire of doing right. . ..' In many ways Fanny is the moral conscience of the novel, since all the other characters are shown to be fallible when faced with moral dilemmas, even Edmund himself. The events in the novel are not viewed solely through Fanny's eyes, but it is to her moral viewpoint that we find ourselves led. Whatever the moral implications of acting might be, we feel and judge, along with Fanny, that performing *Lovers' Vows* would be morally wrong *on this occasion*, and Edmund's attempts to justify his own participation fail to convince anyone, least of all himself. Only Fanny 'acts' rightly, and Sir Thomas returns at the moment when her principles are about to give way under outside pressure.

Perhaps this sense of morality is what so many modern readers find unpalatable in Fanny Price, and the novel as a whole. Like Pinocchio in Carlo Collodi's fable we find delight in occasionally ignoring the voice of conscience, but like him we eventually pay for our folly - though not always as much as we deserve. In Jane Austen's novels we see folly reproved and vice punished, and generally this applies to the heroines as well as the minor characters. Fanny, on the other hand is invariably right, and somehow we find this offensive - it seems almost unnatural. But Fanny is not intended as a paragon by her creator. It we choose to see her as one then we have ignored some of the novel's subtlest ironies. Fanny is deficient in many ways. She lacks humour, at first she seems sickly and not particularly attractive; she lacks any artistic accomplishments and can be gushingly naive and sentimental. Jane Austen makes us aware of all these by setting Fanny for contrast against Mary Crawford and the Bertram girls, who are attractive, healthy and talented. These, however, are wordly accomplishments, and Jane Austen, as a Christian, believed these were less important than the spiritual virtues that led to right thinking and right feeling. Fanny is essentially unworldly. Her quiet, secluded existence is almost monastic, and amid the bustle of Mansfield she maintains a quiet dialogue with the 'still, small voice' of her conscience, her invariable guide to what ought to be done, for as we have already seen, to Jane Austen, every act, however trivial - like deciding whether to return to an estate or not - has a moral significance.

3.2 CHANGE AND IMPROVEMENT

The word 'improvement' occurs frequently in the novel, and its use underlines one of Jane Austen's central concerns – the values of change as opposed to stability. Such an issue, with all the *moral* implications it raises, would have been of great concern to a generation feeling the changes brought about by the French and Industrial Revolutions, but it is just as relevant in the twentieth century, whether we are considering political and social change, or the kinds of change that can occur in individual human beings. All these are examined in *Mansfield Park*, but we must be clear that Jane Austen makes a distinction between change for its own sake, and improvement which implies a necessary change for the better. 'Improvement' to her contemporaries was also a specific term used to describe the alterations made to country houses and their grounds by landscape architects like Capability Brown and his successor Humphrey Repton (who is mentioned in Chapter 6 of the novel). A close reading of *Mansfield Park* reveals that Jane Austen is primarily concerned with two kinds of improvement – material or physical, and moral – and that the two are frequently linked.

One of the central episodes in the novel depicts a visit to Sotherton made by all the young people, ostensibly to discuss possible improvements to the house and grounds. Like its owner, Mr Rushworth, the house is in desperate need of some changes for the better – 'I never saw a place that wanted so much improvement', says Mr Rushworth in Chapter 6, but he is unable to see what improvements are needed. In his own case an infusion of common sense would not be amiss, but the idea of improving Sotherton is taken up by the others. Mrs Norris, who enjoys bustle and innovation, thinks that everything should be arranged in the best style, regardless of expense. Mrs Grant believes that Sotherton would be improved by the presence of Maria Bertram as its mistress, and without the distraction provided by Henry Crawford one cannot help feeling that the latter would have undertaken the complete reformation of both house and owner. Lady Bertram is only concerned that the improvements should include the provision of a shrubbery – one of her favourite spots for resting in hot weather. Henry Crawford is in favour of improvements, in fact he regrets that he has already improved his own estate and can no longer be busy. It is only later that we discover his improvements have not actually benefited his tenants. Mary Crawford objects to improvements because, in the past, she was inconvenienced by some of Admiral Crawford's. Fanny is saddened by the thought that existing natural beauties, like the avenue, will be destroyed. Her feelings are on the side of history, tradition and the status quo, and she must learn the value of improvements for herself - that some changes are necessary. On this occasion it is Edmund who summarises the case most satisfactorily - Sotherton is in need of some improvements, but this should not be undertaken out of a desire to ape current fashions, but to make the house pleasant and habitable for the owner, who should shape it to suit his own needs.

Broadly speaking, we could say that the various characters at this stage in the novel fall into two opposing groups - those like Henry Crawford and Tom Bertram, who look forward to any kind of change in order to provide a distraction from things remaining as they are, and those like Sir Thomas and Fanny, who seem to oppose any kind of change. Of course, neither extreme is acceptable, and during the novel Jane Austen shows her characters coming to terms with changes in themselves and the world around them.

At the centre of the 'improvement' question lies Mansfield itself - the house and grounds. When Fanny first sees the house, as a child, it seems to be cold and forbidding, but gradually she begins to find a niche for herself within the walls, and under the stern supervision of Sir Thomas, Mansfield appears as a symbol of stability - conservative, orthodox, hierarchical, upholding all the social and moral proprieties - everything calm and well-ordered. A park is an area of land enclosed from the outside, but Mansfield is under threat from changes that could undermine its stability.

Its greatest threat comes from the Crawfords, who possess a very different moral outlook from Sir Thomas. Their laxity is soon made clear to us by Henry's mocking attitude towards marriage (he will eventually elope with a married woman) and by Mary's coarse remarks about her uncle, the Admiral, and her later attacks on clergymen. They seem to have been infected by the atheistic and anti-authoritarian ideas of the French Revolution, and their influence is soon apparent on the Bertram children. We learn about Mary's religious views from her remarks in the chapel at Sotherton. Mrs Rushworth tells her visitors that family prayers were discontinued by the late Mr Rushworth, and Mary comments: 'Every age has its improvements.' Fanny watches with mounting horror as Maria is led astray by Henry's flattery and Edmund's judgement is blunted by his infatuation for Mary - all of which leads to the performance of *Lovers' Vows*. Sir Thomas believes that the problem has been solved by burning copies of the play, but at the end of the novel the elopement of his daughters, and the illness of his dissolute son finally bring home the extent of the moral disintegration that has undermined his authority. Only with the marriage of Edmund and Fanny, and the reformation of Tom and Julia is order reaffirmed.

But that is too simple and straightforward for such a subtle artist as Jane Austen, and she also shows that change, or rather improvement is necessary if Mansfield is to survive. Indeed, unless there had been something fundamentally wrong within the house, the Crawfords would not have been so successful. The fault lies, basically, in the kind of authority wielded by Sir Thomas. He is shown as a man who 'thinks rightly' on all occasions, but he has never really considered the human heart in his calculations. He has a kindly nature, but never displays affection, and this has prevented him from really understanding the hearts and dispositions of his children. They have been brought up in the practices of Christianity, but, apart from Edmund, have not developed any moral principles.

> Something must have been wanting *within*, or time would have worn away much of its ill effect. He feared that principle, active principle, had been wanting; that they had never been properly taught to govern their inclinations and tempers by that sense of duty which can alone suffice. They had been instructed theoretically in their religion, but never required to bring it into daily practice. To be distinguished for elegance and accomplishments – the authorised object of their youth – could have had no useful influence that way, no moral effect on the mind. He had meant them to be good, but his cares had been directed to the understanding and manners, not the disposition; and of the necessity of self-denial and humility he feared they had never heard from any lips that could profit them.
>
> (Chapter 48)

Sir Thomas realises his own faults, and we are given the distinct impression at the end of the novel that in the future Mansfield will be ruled with affection as well as justice.

The moral health of Mansfield is renewed by improvements in the condition of its inhabitants. Sir Thomas's eyes have been opened to the bad influence of Mrs Norris, and she leaves the house for ever. Edmund is no longer deceived by Mary, and Tom becomes more useful to his father as he regains moral and physical health. Julia's husband becomes 'less trifling', and there is some hope that their marriage will be a success. Lady Bertram will presumably remain much the same.

Fanny, too, has improved - not in moral, but in physical well-being. Just as she, and other members of her family provide new and healthy supporters of the Mansfield way of life, so the calm, ordered existence exemplified by the house transforms Fanny, and later her sister Susan, into a healthy and attractive young lady. Sir Thomas first realises how much she has improved on his return from Antigua, and later Fanny suffers badly in health and complexion when she is removed to her parents' home in Portsmouth. She needs Mansfield in order to lead a fulfilled and useful life, but the house needs the virtues of Fanny, Susan and William Price - self-denial and humility - in order to continue to exert its influence on everything 'within [its] view and patronage'. The kinds of changes feared on the arrival of the little girl at the beginning of the novel have turned out to be improvements.

3.3 EDUCATION AND UPBRINGING

Fanny is undoubtedly 'improved' by her years at Mansfield, and Jane Austen is interested in examining the nature of the changes that occur in characters through the education and upbringing they receive. In the novel we are presented with contrasted forms of education and home environments, and asked to judge their results for ourselves.

In Jane Austen's age all young men from wealthy families were given a 'classical' education (Latin and Greek) by private tutors, or at public schools, and later at a university. This is true of Tom and Edmund Bertram, and Henry Crawford. William Price, like his younger brothers, would have received a more rudimentary education at a local school. More will be said about professions in section 3.5, but suffice it to say that this classical grounding would have been considered sufficient for elder sons like Henry and Tom, who would inherit their father's property. Edmund must undertake further studies in order to prepare him for ordination.

As we have already seen, Jane Austen's own education, for a young lady of her times, was remarkably broad, and her comment in a letter that she was 'the most unlearned and uninformed female who ever dared to be an authoress' does not do her justice. Her vocabulary was broad, her written style was exquisite, she had read a wide range of books and was clearly well-informed on current affairs. She had not received a sound 'classical' education, but she did possess very sensible views on the kind of education that would benefit young ladies.

Maria and Julia Bertram have a governess, and when Fanny arrives at Mansfield she is expected to take her lessons with them. They soon discover that she is 'prodigiously stupid' because she cannot put together a geographical jigsaw of Europe or recite the principal rivers in Russia. Maria and Julia's own educational acquirements include knowing all the names of the Roman emperors and 'all the metals, semi-metals, planets, and distinguished philosophers'. Fanny is also condemned by them for not wanting to learn music and drawing.

It is clear from these comments that Jane Austen is questioning the traditional notions of what should constitute a young lady's education – a smattering of useless facts (the kind of 'factual' education that Charles Dickens was to attack later in *Hard Times*), and being able to display various accomplishments like singing and painting, the main purpose of which was to attract possible suitors. Jane Austen, like many modern educators, believed that education should be concerned with shaping the mind and the character, and in Fanny, who is aided by Edmund, we see its results, for Fanny reveals later in the novel, as for example when she asks Sir Thomas about the slave trade, that she does not lack information on relevant subjects, is well-read, and interested in the world around her. Thanks to Edmund, and her own perseverance, Fanny's education continues long after the departure of the Mansfield governess, and this is effectively symbolised by the fact that her chosen room in the house should be the old school room. During her time at Portsmouth Fanny undertakes to improve the mind of her younger sister by providing books and encouraging the appreciation of them. In doing this she effectively passes on some of the help given to her by Edmund.

Jane Austen is also concerned that there should be a religious element in education for both sexes. Some of this should be the responsibility of the ordained minister of the Church, which will be discussed below, but it is also the duty of parents in a Christian nation – hence the importance, for Jane Austen, of family worship. Education without moral or religious guidance would be as fruitless as attending religious services without listening to their content. This, though, has been so with the Bertram girls and the Crawfords. Mary Crawford has suffered from being the favourite of her aunt – just as Maria, and to a lesser extent Julia, have been spoilt by Aunt Norris – and her upbringing is largely responsible for her attitudes and manner of speaking:

'Do not you think', said Fanny, after a little consideration, 'that this impropriety is a reflection itself upon Mrs Crawford, as her niece has been entirely brought up by her? She cannot have given her right notions of what was due to the Admiral.'   (Chapter 7)

Upbringing is most important as a theme in the novel because it not only includes education, but the responsibility of parents and guardians to exercise the right kind of authority in establishing a home environment in which children stand a chance of improving their minds and bodies. Apart from glimpses we are given of the Crawfords' upbringing, two households are considered in depth – Mansfield itself, and the home of Fanny's parents in Portsmouth.

The virtues of Mansfield are enumerated in Chapter 39:

> At Mansfield no sounds of contention, no raised voice, no abrupt bursts, no tread of violence, was ever heard; all proceeded in a regular course of cheerful orderliness; everybody had their due importance; everybody's feelings were consulted. If tenderness could be ever supposed wanting, good sense and good breeding supplied its place.

Jane Austen pinpoints with unerring accuracy one of the failings (lack of tenderness) and many of the virtues of Mansfield which help to 'improve' the young Fanny Price – in particular 'good sense and good breeding'. We might also add good food and plenty of healthy exercise in the park. Through her upbringing at Mansfield Fanny becomes a young lady who is fit to take her place in society – she is even given her own 'coming-out' ball. Though lacking the feminine accomplishments of Maria and Julia, she becomes their equal – in the eyes of Heny Crawford, at least – and in her principles she certainly makes up for not being able to paint or play the piano. Where were those principles acquired, for Edmund recognises them already in the young Fanny?

At first we would be inclined to reply that they could not have been learnt in the home of her parents which:

> was the abode of noise, disorder, and impropriety. Nobody was in their right place, nothing was done as it ought to be. She [Fanny] could not respect her parents, as she had hoped.   (Chapter 39)

Yet this upbringing has produced William and Susan (as well as Fanny herself) and their worth is stressed on several occasions. On his first appearance William displays 'proof of good principles', and Fanny is surprised that Susan 'brought up in the midst of negligence and error . . .

should have formed such proper opinions of what ought to be' without the help of someone like Edmund. What Portsmouth has, in fact, taught them is, as Sir Thomas later realises, 'the advantages of early hardship and discipline, and the consciousness of being born to struggle and endure'. We later realise that, despite chaos at home, the Prices remain regular church attenders. They lack the refinements of manners that Mansfield encourages, but Fanny and Susan manage to acquire them, and William appears anything but coarse and uncouth beside Henry Crawford and Tom Bertram. Social 'improvement' is important in the bringing up of children, but in the final balance, as far as Jane Austen is concerned, it weighs less than 'right thinking' and 'right feeling'.

Mansfield Park begins with a discussion about the problems that will be incurred in undertaking the care of Fanny, and through much of the novel we are aware that the major characters divide into two main categories – the 'young people' and those who are responsible for their welfare. Jane Austen is equally critical of those who offer inadequate guidance and those who refuse to acknowledge any restraint on their own personal inclinations. This applies not just within the home, but in society as a whole.

3.4 THE ROLE OF THE CLERGYMAN

In a letter to her sister Cassandra, Jane Austen wrote that her new novel – *Mansfield Park* – would be about 'ordination', a subject on which she was well-informed, with so many ordained clergymen in her own family. We learn by the end of Chapter 2 that Edmund Bertram is to be a clergyman, and from time to time we are informed of his progress, and, in addition, several important discussions with the Crawfords are reported, in which the function of the clergyman is discussed.

Mary only learns of Edmund's choice of career on the visit to Sotherton when, in the chapel, she makes one of her usual remarks in bad taste. Despite her embarrassment, she returns to the topic on leaving the house. Her dislike of the profession is made very clear, and although she accepts Edmund's plea of being a younger son she insists on regarding the clergyman as 'nothing'. Edmund springs to the defence of the ordained minister who 'has the guardianship of religion and morals, and consequently of the manners which result from their influence'. This remark establishes the importance of ordination as a theme, since like a parent with a child, the clergyman, ideally speaking, is the agent responsible for the 'improvement' of society as a whole. Mary misunderstands what Edmund is saying. How can a clergyman, who is only heard once a week, 'govern the conduct and fashion the manners of a large congregation'? Edmund replies by admitting that London is an exception – but maintains that the country clergyman, who will meet his parishioners regularly, is not concerned with their social behaviour, but their moral health:

> The *manners* I speak of might rather be called *conduct*, perhaps, the result of good principles; the effect, in short, of those doctrines which it is their duty to teach and recommend; and it will, I believe, be everywhere found, that as the clergy are or are not what they ought to be, so are the rest of the nation.   (Chapter 9)

Once again, the word 'principle' should alert us to Jane Austen's central concern. Just as the stability of Mansfield is threatened by new influences and short-sighted guardianship, so the moral health of the nation depends on the guidance of God's ordained ministers. In both cases 'good principles' – right thinking, right feeling – are sadly wanting.

In Chapter 25 the position of the clergyman in society is linked to the related theme of house improvements. Henry wants to see Edmund's future home at Thornton Lacey turned into a fashionable country house, with careful improvements, just as his sister would like to see Edmund as a society figure rather than a poor clergyman. Edmund, on the other hand, is content as long as the house gives 'the air of a gentleman's residence' and is comfortable to live in. He also reiterates his own, and Sir Thomas's, view that a clergyman should be resident in his parish in order adequately to provide for the needs of his flock.

To counterpoint her argument Jane Austen provides us with an example of a bad clergyman in Dr Grant – whose inadequacies are listed by Mary Crawford in discussion with Fanny and Edmund. Dr Grant is not ignorant or uncouth – as many eighteenth-century clergyman had been – but he is short-tempered gluttonous and totally oblivious to the spiritual needs of those around him. He preaches his weekly sermon, but smiles on the loose morals of Mary and Henry who are residents, ironically, under his roof. Edmund cannot defend his conduct, but Fanny manages to point out that preaching a weekly sermon must surely encourage some form of moral improvement in the preacher himself! It is highly fitting that Mansfield Parsonage should eventually become the home of Fanny and Edmund.

3.5 THE VALUE OF BEING USEFULLY EMPLOYED

Edmund, with Fanny as his wife, will make an ideal clergyman, but this is not the only profession examined in *Mansfield Park*. The strength of any society depends on all its members fulfilling their functions to the best of their ability, and self-indulgent idleness can be dangerous. This is most emphatically true of Tom Bertram, Henry Crawford and Mr Yates, who spend their time pleasing themselves – the only dread being boredom. Nevertheless, Tom and Henry should be concerned with one role – that of being a landowner. The latter possesses an estate already, and the former will eventually inherit Mansfield, but neither fully understands what the management or improvement of an estate really involves, and the eighteenth century had seen many advances in the science of agriculture. Not only was a landowner responsible for the land itself, but a good one was concerned with the crops and the welfare of all those who rented or worked the land. A landowner, like Henry, who was absent for most of the year was as bad for the estate as an absentee clergyman for his parish. Sir Thomas takes his position very seriously – as we see when he wastes no time in getting back to work on his return from Antigua, which he had visited in order to supervise other estates. Tom eventually learns to be useful to his father, and Henry, influenced by Fanny, considers the happiness of his tenants, but for most of the novel they are only concerned with country sports and amusing pastimes. They try to employ their time, but they only succeed in being busy – often to no effect. 'Let us be doing something,' says Henry, and the result is *Lovers' Vows*. Later he reminisces to Fanny about the rehearsals: 'There was employment, hope, solicitude, bustle for every hour of the day.'

A great distinction is made in the novel between being usefully employed and being busy to no purpose. Girls of Jane Austen's class did not work in the modern sense of the word – unless financial difficulties drove them into seeking employment as a governess or companion – but with them, too, being employed is important. Fanny is generally working at one task or another – running errands for Lady Bertram, sewing for the poor and reading to improve her mind. Mrs Norris is always busy and occupied, yet her usefulness is confined primarily to herself, and her eventual departure from Mansfield is mourned by nobody. At the other extreme is Lady Bertram, who spends her entire life doing nothing.

Those who are usefully employed, whether domestically or in the world outside, benefit from the hard work and self-discipline that are needed. If Henry had returned to Everingham, the decision to do his duty by his tenants would have necessarily involved giving up the pleasures of London society and the chance of meeting Maria. Self-denial, which has never been encouraged by his upbringing – he has been spoilt by the Admiral – proves too much for him. Like Mr Yates, Henry has little to recommend him but 'habits of fashion and expense' while his sister can say: 'Nothing ever fatigues me but doing what I do not like.' The Crawfords, the Bertram girls and Tom have all been spoilt by an over-indulgent upbringing.

Of course, grinding poverty and endless toil are not recommended as a viable alternative. In Chapter 7 Fanny is deprived of healthy, outdoor recreation, when Mary monopolises her pony, and is needlessly over-employed by her two aunts. The result is that Fanny nearly collapses. The Price household is shown as an unhealthy environment, and the task of trying to set it right has been too much for Susan:

> Susan tried to be useful, where *she* [Fanny] could only have gone away and cried; and that Susan was useful she could perceive; that things, bad as they were, would have been worse but for such interposition, and that both her mother and Betsey were restrained from some excesses of very offensive indulgence and vulgarity.
>
> (Chapter 40)

Notice once again, in this passage, how Jane Austen's message is reiterated by the use of key words that occur throughout the novel – 'useful', 're-strained', 'indulgence'.

Fanny makes herself useful as much as her retiring character will allow – sewing for her brothers, and trying to improve Susan's mind and character. The latter is highly successful, and Susan takes Fanny's place as Lady Bertram's companion, having 'an inclination for usefulness'. A careful reading of the novel will reveal how fully Fanny uses her time, and the description of her own room (Chapter 16) helps us to understand the nature of her occupations.

The best example of someone usefully employed, and in a chosen career, is William Price. Because of her family involvement, Jane Austen had a high opinion of the navy, and William is shown to possess all the qualities that make an excellent naval officer. On his first arrival at Mansfield he displays 'proof of good principles, professional knowledge, energy, courage, and cheerfulness – everything that could deserve or promise well'. William is not one of the uncouth, illiterate officers that can be found in the novels of the eighteenth-century writer Tobias Smollett, but, like Jane

TO24285

Austen's brothers, an intelligent, well-mannered sailor with a sound moral backbone. He makes a great impression on Henry Crawford, for in his short time at sea William has displayed heroism and endured much: 'The glory of heroism, of usefulness, of exertion, of endurance, made his own habits of selfish indulgence appear in shameful contrast.' At the end of the novel we hear of William's 'continued good conduct and rising fame'. Once again, the patronage of Mansfield – in furthering his career – has paid dividends, for the house, like the nation, will only endure if it is protected from its enemies, both foreign and domestic.

3.6 MARRIAGE

Since Jane Austen's chosen subject was the social behaviour of that portion of the life of the gentry which was accessible to women, it is hardly surprising that marriage is an important theme in all her novels. For ladies of her time and class, marriage was the most crucial event in their lives, for it determined their future economic and social status, as well as their personal happiness. Jane Austen once wrote in a letter that marriage was 'a great improver', and in the above context it is easy to see why, but the phrase serves to remind us yet again that the moral debate on 'improvement' is still present when we consider why marriages take place.

The opening paragraph of the novel describes the very different marriages of the three Ward sisters, and we learn more about them as we read on. Maria Ward has the 'good luck' to marry Sir Thomas Bertram. She has greatly improved her financial position, and her luck lies in the fact that Lady Bertram has little to recommend her apart from good looks. The marriage is essentially one built on wealth and position rather than strong feeling. Miss Ward, the eldest sister, marries Mr Norris, we infer, from a sense of desperation at being left on the shelf, since it is not a marriage built on wealth or love. We read that she 'found herself obliged to be attached' to her husband, and on his subsequent death we are told that 'Mrs Norris . . . consoled herself for the loss of her husband by considering that she could do very well without him.' The third sister, Mrs Price, has made an imprudent marriage because she has allowed her feelings to overpower her judgement, and she ends up with too little money and too many children to bring up on it.

We are shown many bad or 'unequal' marriages in *Mansfield Park*, and the disastrous consequences are made clear, particularly when we consider the upbringing of children. Admiral Crawford's unhappy domestic life has scarred Henry and Mary for life, souring their own attitude to marriage. Lady Bertram and Sir Thomas never display much affection, and when this is compounded by the former's indolence, the result is damaging to their children. Mrs Norris, having been an unfeeling wife, becomes an over-indulgent aunt – still lacking real affection. Mr and Mrs Price achieve very limited success in bringing up their own children. Maria Bertram's marriage ends in divorce. Dr and Mrs Grant are ill matched in age and temperament. Fortunately the last two do not produce offspring.

Good marriages, as far as Jane Austen is concerned, depend on there being an 'equality' in the relationship between the man and the woman – what might be seen as a balance between right thinking and right feeling. Nothing was worse than marrying without affection, on the other hand it would be foolish to marry without adequate means of support. Lady Bertram tells Fanny that it is a woman's duty to improve her position by marrying a rich man, but she is blind to the fact that other kinds of improvement can take place through marriage.

At the centre of each of Jane Austen's novels we are shown a young couple who possess all the requirements for a successful marriage, and this novel is no exception.

Fanny is given a chance to improve her social and financial position, and that of her brothers and sisters, by marrying Henry Crawford, but it is clear that they are unequal in many ways. Although Fanny is Sir Thomas's niece, she is Henry's social inferior. The fact that Henry is prepared to accept this comes as a surprise to Fanny, and his regard for her enables him to talk to Mr Price without condescension. Morally speaking, Fanny is Henry's superior, but he admits this, and once again the amount of improvement that has taken place in Henry surprises us. Temperamentally they are very different, but it is Edmund who tries to persuade Fanny that this is of little importance.

> I am perfectly persuaded that the tempers had better be unlike; I mean unlike in the flow of the spirits, in the manners, in the inclination for much or little company, in the propensity to talk or to be silent, to be grave or to be gay. Some opposition here is, I am thoroughly convinced, friendly to matrimonial happiness.
>
> (Chapter 35)

If we also take into account Fanny and Henry's mutual enjoyment of literature, there is some reason for believing that, with the latter's continuing improvement, a marriage between them would not have been a complete failure, and clearly this is a notion which the author herself wished her readers to entertain. Only two strong reasons convince us otherwise.

First, having seen Henry's behaviour with Maria, and knowing what a consummate actor he is, we cannot help doubting whether his moral regeneration is complete. Mary's last interview with Edmund reveals *her* thoughts on the probable conclusion of a marriage between Fanny and her brother:

> Had she accepted him as she ought, they might now have been on the point of marriage, and Henry would have been too happy and too busy to want any other object. He would have taken no pains to be on terms with Mrs Rushworth again. It would have all ended in a regular standing flirtation, in yearly meetings at Sotherton and Everingham. (Chapter 47)

One cannot imagine the possibility of Fanny being happy in a situation like that.

Secondly, Fanny is in love with Edmund. This is made apparent at the end of Chapter 2, and the way she fights to suppress her jealousy of Mary convinces us that, though quiet, her feelings for him are strong. Despite Sir Thomas's fears of Fanny's marrying one of her cousins, we soon realise - long before Edmund himself - that he and Fanny are ideally suited. They are temperamentally the same, and they share a similar outlook on life - Edmund has helped to form Fanny's mind himself. Socially, Fanny has proved acceptable to Sir Thomas, and the two of them will be financially secure, without owning tremendous wealth. Edmund has always loved Fanny as a sister, and now that his eyes have been opened to Mary Crawford's true character, the way is clear for him to view her as a wife.

One critic has commented that an evening at the Parsonage with Mr and Mrs Edmund Bertram would prove rather dull - perhaps so. But in making this comment the critic concerned is falling into the same error as those who can only regard Fanny as a prig. She and Edmund are not remarkable people, and Jane Austen's ending makes this clear. Mary Crawford and her brother are undoubtedly more entertaining, and marriage with either of them would have proved full of variety, but our attention as readers is directed towards the humbler virtues that stand high on the moral scale:

> With so much true merit and true love, and no want of fortune or friends, the happiness of the married cousins must appear as

secure as earthly happiness can be. Equally formed for domestic life, and attached to country pleasures, their home was the home of affection and comfort. . . .   (Chapter 48)

From whatever point we begin our examination of the novel, we almost always find that we return to the question of 'morals', and this is hardly surprising, for even in her 'sparkling' novels Jane Austen is essentially a moralist, ridiculing those aspects of human behaviour that can and should be changed.

4 TECHNICAL FEATURES

4.1 PLOT AND STRUCTURE

The plot of the novel is essentially a simple one, and has been compared to the fairy story *Cinderella* in the way that a poor girl wins her Prince Charming. Chapter 1 begins with an account of the events that lead up to Fanny's arrival at Mansfield, and Chapter 48 ends with her as mistress of Mansfield Parsonage. Like a conventional fairy story, the novel opens with a traditional flourish, which might be paraphrased, 'Once upon a time there were three sisters', and ends with the married couple living happily ever after. This broad pattern can be found in Jane Austen's other novels, and it is a formula which provides the reader with a great deal of satisfaction.

As with a traditional fairy story the reader is kept in a certain amount of suspense as to the eventual outcome. Despite the many entertaining diversions en route, the most important question in the reader's mind is: Will Fanny marry Edmund? Because Jane Austen is a writer of ironic comedy, a happy ending is expected, but her skill ensures that it is never entirely certain, and events are continually altering our expectations – Edmund's kindness over the pony is followed by Mary's appropriation of it, his gift of a necklace by his eulogies of Mary's own kindness to Fanny. Henry's proposal, and Fanny's trip to Portsmouth, seem to destroy any possibility of her marrying Edmund, and it is only Tom's illness that prevents him writing a proposal to Mary. Convention, and her own natural timidity, do not allow Fanny to tell Edmund what she feels, and this adds more uncertainty, particularly for the modern reader who feels that everything would be so simple if only Fanny would tell Edmund the truth about her love for him.

Although the basic plot is simple, the various themes of the novel add to its complexity, for Fanny's love for Edmund is not Jane Austen's only concern. Events must follow each other in a sequence, but not every one can be of equal importance. The novel must *appear* to be as random as life itself, but actually possess its own inexorable logic. It must give the impression of time passing while eliminating those minutes, hours and even years that do not directly concern the reader.

Fanny's arrival at Mansfield occurs when she is ten, and her marriage at approximately nineteen (we cannot be certain how long it took Edmund to forget Mary!), but it is clear to readers by Chapter 3 that the novel does not attempt anything near a chronological survey of the years in between. R.W. Chapman has shown, in an appendix to his Oxford Illustrated edition of the novel, that Jane Austen probably made use of an almanac when writing *Mansfield Park*, and that five months pass between the ball (Chapter 28) and Edmund's account of his last interview with Mary (Chapter 47) - nearly half the novel. By working backwards we discover that Fanny was eighteen when the Crawfords arrived at the Parsonage (Chapter 4), so that most of the novel is concerned with events in Fanny's life over a period of about ten months, but this is narrowed still further by Jane Austen's skill in condensing days or weeks in which little of interest occurs, in order to concentrate on episodes that are of great significance.

The important episodes are the outing to Sotherton (Chapter 9-10), the rehearsal of *Lovers' Vows* (13-20), the ball (26-28), Henry Crawford's proposal (30-36), and Fanny's visit to Portsmouth (38-46). To a certain extent each of these is self-contained. The first and last are defined by the journeys they involve. The rehearsals begin with the arrival of Mr Yates, and all reminders of them are removed with his subsequent departure. Chapter 26 begins with Sir Thomas planning the ball, while Chapter 28 ends with Fanny leaving it to go to bed. Henry's wish to marry Fanny is revealed to his sister on his return from London, and although his courtship of her continues at Portsmouth, the episode is brought to an emphatic conclusion at the end of Chapter 36: 'On the morrow the Crawfords were gone.'

Despite the importance of these episodes Jane Austen ensures that they do not fragment the novel, by skilfully overlapping at the beginning and end of them. For example, although the young people arrive at Sotherton in Chapter 9, the previous chapter describes their journey as well as some of the preparations for it, while the original discussions on improving the house occurred in Chapter 6. Even greater overlaps occur in Chapter 37, where Jane Austen manages to include an extra subject of interest for the reader – whether Mrs Norris will accompany Fanny and William. One particular chapter (25) contains an important minor episode – the game of 'Speculation', but it is the longer ones that most impress themselves on the reader.

Mansfield Park was originally published in three volumes (Chapters 1–18, 19–31 and 32–48) and the breaks, too, occur at important moments. Jane Austen exploits the form in order to shock the reader with the sudden return of Sir Thomas (Chapter 18), and later to leave the reader in momentary suspense at the outcome of Henry's proposal (Chapter 31). Further moments of surprise occur when Henry suddenly reveals his love for Fanny, while suspense is heightened by uncertainty over Henry's improvement – will Fanny accept him? – and Edmund's infatuation for Mary – will his eyes be opened before it is too late?

Much of the third volume creates suspense by removing Fanny from events at Mansfield and London. Not only does this increase the reader's sense of Fanny's helplessness and isolation, but it also allows Jane Austen to avoid narrating scenes that she might have encountered difficulty in handling, for example Maria's elopement. Letters play an important part in the construction of the Portsmouth scenes, and their use reminds us that some of Jane Austen's favourite novelists used a series of letters to provide the structure for an entire novel – as she herself did in *Lady Susan*, written before *Mansfield Park*, and in some of her juvenile works.

Throughout the novel our attention is focused on events as they affect Fanny – despite occasional revelations of what the Crawfords are saying, or plotting – but the title of the book could never be her name as with the heroine of *Emma*. *Mansfield Park* is about the house as well as the heroine; indeed it is about both of them, for even at Portsmouth Fanny is thinking about the house that has become a 'home' for her. Each of the episodes has a double significance, therefore, affecting individuals, and the general life of the house. The behaviour of the young people at Sotherton reflects on their own faults, but also makes us aware of the threats to Mansfield. In these social encounters Fanny provides a useful centre for our attention by remaining the only stable point in a series of changes. As we learn more about Fanny we also get to know the house and its ways. We are never given any elaborate description of the outside, but we are aware of its size, its sense of order and dignified atmosphere. We know the names of the various servants and their functions. Tom and Edmund go shooting in its woods, Fanny cuts roses in the flower garden, Lady Bertram dozes in the shrubbery and Mrs Norris bustles to and from the Parsonage or the White House – the former 'gently rising beyond the village road'. The life of the house is made very real for us.

In this sense, therefore, the structure of the entire novel depends on the setting which provides its title. Jane Austen does not go as far as some later novelists by making the house the most important element in the story, a kind of inanimate hero, but the story of Fanny Price is made richer and more complex by its presence.

4.2 CHARACTERISATION

Over fifty fictional characters are named, and their variety and richness of description help to establish the world of the novel as 'real' and vital. Of the central characters, like Fanny, Edmund and the Crawfords, we learn a great deal. Less important ones like Mr Price or Lady Bertram are not as fully developed, and we tend to remember one particular aspect of their character. But even very minor characters, whose names occur only once in the entire novel, are given identities which have some bearing on the major themes.

Consider, for example, Miss Lee, the governess at Mansfield. Her name appears in the first chapter when Mrs Norris remarks that it will be just the same to her 'whether she has three girls to teach, or only two'. Later we discover that she has acted as a companion to Lady Bertram, and been no longer required when the Bertram girls have reached the age of matrimony. She has wondered at Fanny's ignorance, but left her the legacy of the schoolroom. All of which adds up to very little information, but nevertheless a recognisable 'type' which the author allows us to 'flesh out' for ourselves. We can deduce very clearly that Miss Lee (poor, but educated) has had to put up with unpleasantness from Mrs Norris - something else that Fanny inherits from her, as well as the duty of running around after Lady Bertram which up till now has been the prerogative of Miss Lee. We can also infer that Miss Lee had little chance of controlling Maria and Julia, who would have regarded her as a kind of servant. No one who has read any novels by Charlotte or Anne Brontë can have any illusions about the life of a governess. Miss Lee plays a significant part in the lives of those at Mansfield, but even the absence of those with no great significance - like Mr Price's drinking companion, Old Scholey, or Maddison, Mr Crawford's agent - would diminish our sense of the novel's richness.

In depicting more important characters Jane Austen has a variety of means at her disposal. Sometimes we are given a brief pen-portrait by the narrator, to direct us towards one aspect of that character's behaviour. Of Lady Bertram we are informed that she 'was a woman of very tranquil feelings, and a temper remarkably easy and indolent', and our subsequent impressions of her behaviour only add to this initial one. Mr Rushworth and Mr Yates are introduced in a similar way. Jane Austen frequently uses her privilege as a narrator to allow her readers a glimpse of what is going on in a person's mind – usually thoughts or feelings that would not be revealed under normal circumstances, for example Tom's 'justification' of his behaviour in Chapter 3, or Mary Crawford's state of mind concerning Edmund in Chapter 29. Such revelations are very important in our own understanding of Fanny, given her shy, reticent nature, and the fact that for most of the novel her main confidant, Edmund, cannot be consulted on the subject that concerns her most deeply.

We can also learn about certain characters from what they say, and their manner of speaking. Each of the major characters is given a recognisable tone, to which we can instantly respond, but this is even truer of minor characters. Mr Price makes his first impression on us as a voice rather than a figure, while Mr Rushworth's vacancy is suggested by the way his first speech reiterates the phrase 'I do not know'. In the case of the Crawfords, our most striking early glimpse of them occurs in Chapter 4 where after a token description – 'Henry, though not handsome, had air and countenance' – we are given a sample of their witty, elegant style of speaking, complete with puns and quotations. They are both accomplished talkers, as opposed to Edmund, whose manner of speaking echoes his father – dignified, but occasionally bordering on the pompous. We cannot imagine either of them sounding like Tom, with his 'By Jove! this won't do'.

One of the most distinctive voices in the novel is that of Mrs Norris, and it helps to reinforce what we are told about her behaviour. Her bustling personality is only matched by her ability to dominate any conversation, once her seemingly unending voice has been switched on. In Chapter 20 Sir Thomas is unable to tackle her about the acting because of the barrage of words hurled at him, and Mrs Norris avoids any chance of being reprimanded. Taken out of context we might find Mrs Norris's speech and character totally comic, but Jane Austen, as narrator, makes every effort to inform readers that the flood of words *is* a form of deceit. Beneath her desire to appear helpful and considerate Mrs Norris is only concerned with her own welfare. This outwardly amusing woman has disastrous effects on those around her.

Even Fanny, whose character lies at the very centre of the novel possesses *two* very distinctive speaking voices. Occasionally, her quiet, unobtrusive tone is interrupted by a more enthusiastic and eloquent outpouring

- usually on some aspect of the natural world, for example: 'Here's harmony . . . here's repose! Here's what may leave all painting and all music behind, and what poetry can only attempt to describe.' This kind of speech, when added to Jane Austen's narratorial descriptions of Fanny's struggles against her own feelings, helps us to appreciate that beneath her apparently calm exterior Fanny has a romantic and emotional nature.

Much of Jane Austen's characterisation is concerned with peeling away the layers of veneer that people use to present the world with a certain image of themselves. Whether by direct authorial revelation, or indirectly through what they say, the men and women in *Mansfield Park* are shown for what they really are, despite their outward circumstances. Lady Bertram and Mrs Price are both inadequate mothers, but the inadequacy lies in their characters rather than their surroundings, which only serve to heighten the defect of indolence. Edmund deceives himself into believing that Mary's faults are to be found in her outward behaviour - her cruel sense of humour, her selfishness - whereas, in truth, they lie much deeper, in her total inability to distinguish between right and wrong. Mary's tragedy, and that of her brother, is that they *do* wish to change their personalities but are unable to do so - only their outward behaviour can be modified.

Jane Austen cannot reveal the psychological complexities of some twentieth-century novelists, but within the limitations of her time, she possesses the skill to portray three-dimensional rather than cardboard characters. One of her favourite novelists was Samuel Richardson, who managed to create great complexity in his fictional characters by allowing us to glimpse their minds in action through the letters they write to different correspondents. Similarly, Jane Austen, by grouping and re-grouping her fictional characters, allowing them to comment on each other's behaviour, and by only intervening when the reader is liable to miss the point, is able to create believable human beings who develop, change and surprise us.

All the central characters are allowed to change and develop. We see Fanny learning fundamental truths about herself from her experiences at Portsmouth, and Edmund's judgement being gradually undermined by the influence of Mary Crawford. Henry Crawford's behaviour at Portsmouth takes both Fanny and the reader by surprise, and allows us to dally with the possibility that he might prove a good husband after all. Even Lady Bertram surprises us by showing genuine concern for Tom's health. Jane Austen's skill in creating three-dimensional characters, capable of develop-ment, was one of the qualities to attract the attention of her brother

Henry when he read the manuscript of *Mansfield Park*. She wrote to Cassandra, 'I believe *now* he has changed his mind as to foreseeing the end; he said yesterday at least, that he defied anybody to say whether H C (Henry Crawford) would be reformed, or would forget Fanny in a fortnight.'

Mansfield Park is a mature work and shows the author's powers of characterisation at their best. Fictional characters can never be 'real', but they *can* convince us by their resemblance to human beings we meet in our daily lives. Perhaps the final word ought to go to another novelist who learnt much from Jane Austen. In *Aspects of the Novel* (1927), the writer E. M. Forster analyses Lady Bertram in some detail, and concludes that in comparison with Dickens, Jane Austen's characters:

> are more highly organised. They function all round, and even if her plot made greater demands on them than it does they would still be adequate. . . . All the Jane Austen characters are ready for an extended life, for a life which the scheme of her books seldom requires them to lead, and that is why they lead their actual lives so satisfactorily.

4.3 STYLE AND LANGUAGE

In a letter to her niece, Anna, Jane Austen had the following comment to make on one of the former's fictional characters:

> Devereux Forester's being ruined by his Vanity is extremely good; but I wish you would not let him plunge into a 'vortex of Dissipation.' I do not object to the Thing, but I cannot bear the expression; – it is such thorough novel slang – and so old, that I dare say Adam met with it in the first novel he opened.

Jane Austen was to approach her own novel-writing with the same meticulous eye for detail employed in her sewing. No phrase, no word, is deemed as unworthy of her attention. Consider, for example, the way in which she describes one of her own characters entering a 'vortex of Dissipation'. In Chapter 13 Henry Crawford's desire to act is described thus: 'in all the riot of his gratifications it was yet an untasted pleasure'. The last words, with their suggestion of forbidden fruit are well-chosen, but the word 'riot' can appear somewhat extravagant to a modern reader with its overtones of public tumult and disorder, until we turn to the *Shorter Oxford English*

Dictionary and read the following definition: 'Wanton, loose, or wasteful living; debauchery, dissipation, extravagance', and it soon becomes clear that Jane Austen knew precisely what she meant. Careful choice of words can be seen in Mary Crawford's description of marriage as a 'manœuvring business' or the narrator's portrait of Lady Bertram – 'the picture of health, wealth, ease and tranquillity'. How beautifully those adjectives slide off the tongue! – not one can be changed without destroying the total effect. In addition we need only recall Jane Austen's use of words like 'improvement', 'principles', 'employment', to reach the conclusion that using a single sheet of writing-paper at a time must have allowed her to choose her words with infinite care.

The same might be said of the way Jane Austen constructs phrases and sentences. She was a product of the eighteenth century, and despite the publication dates of her novels, her style remains true to the Classical qualities of eighteenth-century writers like Samuel Johnson – moderation, elegance and simplicity. Any page from her novels reveals her adherence to these, and we are made more aware of them by her deliberate lapses. Fanny's outbursts of romantic enthusiasm, for example, or the wonderful parody of inflated newspaper prose in Chapter 46.

Balanced sentences and phrases are used most effectively in those sections where the narrator depicts events or characters, for example in these sentences from the opening paragraphs of Chapter 33:

> He would not despair: he would not desist.
> Fanny knew her meaning, but was no judge of her own manner.
> She must be courteous, and she must be compassionate.

Even in long and more complex sentences Jane Austen's meaning is immediately clear – if we read carefully, with due consideration for the punctuation – and it is remarkable how much matter they convey, as any attempt at paraphrase will reveal.

Such examples abound throughout *Mansfield Park*, and they help to set the tone of the whole novel. Just as there are no great, dramatic events, so the reader never feels that he is being articifially excited by emotional language, 'full of sound and fury'. Characters and events are discussed in a rational manner, and the narrator's voice is that of an educated person indulging in a formal conversation. We must remember that in Jane Austen's day conversation was cultivated as an 'art' in its own right. Henry Crawford's eloquence is a good example of this.

If we detect the speaking voice in the words of Jane Austen's narrator, then it is felt even more strongly in the conversations that dominate the bulk of the novel. The dialogues are as dramatic, in the best sense of the word, as any to be found in plays of the period, with the added advantage that, without any unnecessary rhetoric, they are probably a truer reflection of the language spoken in the drawing-rooms at Chawton and Godmersham.

We have seen how character may be suggested by certain expressions, but the sense we gather of individual speakers also depends on the structure of what they say. In the following speech from Chapter 31 Jane Austen wants to show Fanny's confusion at the news of William's promotion. Her flustered tones are conveyed perfectly by the incomplete sentences and the twice emphasised 'your'.

> Has this been all *your* doing, then?. . . Good Heaven! how very, very kind! Have you really - was it by *your* desire? - I beg your pardon, but I am bewildered. Did Admiral Crawford apply? - how was it? - I am stupefied.

The words 'cried Fanny' in the text have been omitted in this quotation, but an actress playing Fanny would hardly require them - the words speak themselves.

On another occasion, in Chapter 6, we are allowed to hear a very different tone of voice. Mary Crawford is speaking of her naval acquaintances:

> 'Among admirals, large enough; but', with an air of grandeur, 'we know very little of the inferior ranks. Post-captains may be very good sort of men, but they do not belong to *us*.'

The dramatic quality of the language, the way in which snobbery is conveyed through speech, is such that we cringe inwardly at the word 'inferior' and the élitism of '*us*'.

In *Mansfield Park* Jane Austen displays a perfect grasp of the linguistic means necessary to achieve her artistic ends. She lacks the range of many novelists who came after her, and of one or two who came before, but few of them share her skill in depicting the fine and subtle shades of meaning - what Sir Walter Scott called 'the exquisite touch':

4.4 IRONY

In Jane Austen's novels 'irony' is a vital element, indeed we might say that her vision of the world around her is 'ironic'. The word 'irony' implies a reversal of our expectations in what a person says or does, or in the unforeseen outcome of a series of events; and irony as a literary device is used by all the great comic writers. They employ irony to show us the great gulf that lies between how things should be and how they are, between what a person says and what he does, between how he sees himself, and how others see him, what he expects to happen and what does happen, – such contrasts are the raw material of comedy. Jane Austen uses irony to show the true nature that lies behind the faces, or masks, that her various characters present to the world, and to indicate that their intentions are not always fulfilled.

In the opening chapter Mrs Norris, in trying to convince Sir Thomas that Fanny ought to be brought to Mansfield declares that his fears about one of his sons falling in love with their cousin are unfounded, since such a thing is 'morally impossible' if they are brought up together. By the end of the next chapter we are fully aware of Fanny's love for her cousin, and by the end of the novel they are married, and Sir Thomas is overjoyed!

It is even more ironic that Fanny, the outsider in need of assistance, should become one of the mainstays of Mansfield. Sir Thomas, who prides himself on his discernment, only realises her value after the disasters that overtake his own children. Jane Austen notes, in a perceptive comment, that Sir Thomas's realisation 'formed just such a contrast . . . as time is for ever producing between the plans and decisions of mortals, for their own instruction and their neighbours' entertainment'.

Henry Crawford's fate is very ironic. Having been a notorious flirt and breaker of women's hearts, he is eventually caught by the one woman who cannot be wooed by his winning tongue. Even Mary can see the ridiculous nature of his fate, but her own is little better, since having despised poor younger sons and clergymen, she is finally attracted to one who will eventually manage to resist her feminine wiles.

Such large dramatic ironies occur many times in the novel. Characters are shown as unaware of the implications of what they say or do. Edmund tries to persuade Fanny that marriage with Henry would be a sensible step, entirely unaware that she is in love with him; while Henry, a few chapters later, declares to Fanny that 'My conduct shall speak for me!' It does – he elopes with Maria! It is a great irony that Sir Thomas should order the fire to be lit in Fanny's room – thus acknowledging her importance in the household – at the moment when he is most displeased by her behaviour. Fanny only realises on visiting her parents' Portsmouth home that her real 'home' is back at Mansfield. It is deeply ironic that the play chosen by the young people should be *Lovers' Vows*, since during the rehearsals Maria continually hopes for the declaration of love that Henry never makes.

Another kind of irony is to be found on almost every page of the novel in the words spoken by various characters and those used by the narrator. These comments do not rely on any subsequent action, like Henry's remark quoted above, but rather on the reader's knowledge of what a particular character is really like.

Even in the opening sentences Jane Austen's verbal irony can be found, revealing aspects of human behaviour that might otherwise be overlooked. Miss Maria Ward has 'had the good luck to captivate Sir Thomas Bertram'. It has not just been 'good luck' in terms of the chance encounter that brought the two together, or because 'her uncle, the lawyer himself, allowed her to be at least three thousand pounds short of any equitable claim to it'. Maria has the 'good luck' of a pretty face, which has allowed her to 'captivate' a man infinitely her superior in every way. The 'greatness of the match' is measured in financial terms by society, but, as the novel progresses, the reader begins to see only the great disparity there is between husband and wife. Lady Bertram has not 'deserved' her good fortune, having no 'equitable claim' to her husband's love.

Such ironic comments from the narrator are often to be found when new characters are introduced, and we must be made aware of certain defects in their natures. For example, the Crawfords are said to have found a 'kind home' in their uncle's house, whereas their lives have been ruined by the years spent under his roof. Mary Crawford finds that Tom Bertram will suit her since he is the *eldest* son, and his personal attractions are rounded off by a list of what he will inherit – this quickly establishes Mary's mercenary nature, for we now realise the meaning implied in her earlier statement that 'everybody should marry as soon as they can do it to advantage'. The Honourable John Yates (is his title ironic?) is introduced as a man who 'had not much to recommend him beyond habits of fashion and expense', but his habits are, in fact, hardly recommendations.

When we begin to hear these various characters speak for themselves, irony shows what they are actually thinking or feeling. Again in the opening chapter Mrs Norris declares, 'My own trouble, you know, I never regard', but subsequent chapters show that her own interest is usually at the centre of everything she does. In the conversation on improvement Maria reveals much about her attitude to her future husband when she says, 'I really know very little of Sotherton.' Mary states, in Chapter 5, 'I do not know where the error lies.' She is discussing female behaviour with Tom and Edmund, but the judgement draws the reader's attention to her own moral blindness.

Jane Austen reveals the inconsistencies in human behaviour, because, like many comic writers, she is also a moralist, believing that if deception and self-deception were practised less, the world would be a better place. Irony is her sharpest weapon since it serves to expose delusions, in the hope that we may all see a little more clearly. When vice occurs it is openly condemned, but folly is gently mocked and can be amended. The moral purpose of the novel permeates every aspect of Jane Austen's craft, and irony is her tool.

5 EXAMINATION
OF A
SPECIMEN PASSAGE

Even a short extract from the novel can reveal Jane Austen's concern with certain issues, and many features of her technical skill. We must always read a Jane Austen novel with special care to appreciate its many beauties, and the following passage, from Chapter 46, is no exception. The lines have been numbered for easy reference.

The next day came and brought no second letter. Fanny was disappointed. She could still think of little else all the morning; but when her father came back in the afternoon, with the daily newspaper as usual, she was so far from expecting any elucidation through
5   such a channel, that the subject was for a moment out of her head.

She was deep in other musing. The remembrance of her first evening in that room, of her father and his newspaper, came across her. No candle was *now* wanted. The sun was yet an hour and half above the horizon. She felt that she had, indeed, been three months
10   there; and the sun's rays falling strongly into the parlour, instead of cheering, made her still more melancholy; for sunshine appeared to her a totally different thing in a town and in the country. Here, its power was only a glare, a stifling, sickly glare, serving but to bring forward stains and dirt that might otherwise have slept. There was
15   neither health nor gaiety in sunshine in a town. She sat in a blaze of oppressive heat, in a cloud of moving dust; and her eyes could only wander from the walls marked by her father's head, to the table, cut and notched by her brothers, where stood the tea-board never thoroughly cleaned, the cups and saucers wiped in streaks, the milk
20   a mixture of motes floating in thin blue, and the bread and butter growing every minute more greasy than even Rebecca's hands had

first produced it. Her father read his newspaper, and her mother
lamented over the ragged carpet as usual, while the tea was in
preparation, – and wished Rebecca would mend it; and Fanny was
first roused by his calling out to her, after humphing and considering
over a particular paragraph – 'What's the name of your great cousins
in town, Fan?'

A moment's recollection enabled her to say, 'Rushworth, sir.'

'And don't they live in Wimpole Street?'

'Yes, sir.'

'Then, there's the devil to pay among them, that's all. There
(holding out the paper to her) – much good may such fine relations
do you. I don't know what Sir Thomas may think of such matters;
he may be too much of the courtier and fine gentleman to like his
daughter the less. But by G— if she belonged to *me*, I'd give her the
rope's end as long as I could stand over her. A little flogging for man
and woman too would be the best way of preventing such things.'

Fanny read to herself that 'it was with infinite concern the
newspaper had to announce to the world a matrimonial *fracas* in the
family of Mr. R. of Wimpole Street; the beautiful Mrs R., whose
name had not long been enrolled in the lists of Hymen, and who had
promised to become so brilliant a leader in the fashionable world,
having quitted her husband's roof in company with the well-known
and captivating Mr. C., the intimate friend and associate of Mr. R.,
and it was not known, even to the editor of the newspaper, whither
they were gone.'

'It is a mistake, sir,' said Fanny instantly; 'it must be a mistake –
it cannot be true – it must mean some other people.'

She spoke from the instinctive wish of delaying shame, she spoke
with a resolution which sprang from despair, for she spoke what she
did not, could not, believe herself. It had been the shock of conviction as she read. The truth rushed on her; and how she could
have spoken at all, how she could even have breathed, was afterwards matter of wonder to herself.

Mr. Price cared too little about the report to make her much
answer. 'It might be all a lie,' he acknowledged; 'but so many fine
ladies were going to the devil now-a-days that way, that there was no
answering for anybody.'

'Indeed, I hope it is not true,' said Mrs. Price, plaintively, 'it
would be so very shocking! – If I have spoken once to Rebecca
about that carpet, I am sure I have spoke at least a dozen times;
have not I, Betsey? – And it would not be ten minutes' work.'

Fanny, while staying at her parents' home in Portsmouth, has just received a puzzling letter from Mary. Henry's elopement with Maria is confirmed by an oblique reference in the gossip column of Mr Price's newspaper.

The passage moves from Fanny's internal preoccupations to a description of the room, followed by her conversation with Mr Price, Fanny's reading of the newspaper and her reaction to its contents. Finally we hear the comments of Mr and Mrs Price to the news. It is Fanny who dominates the scene, and the narrator wishes us to see the parlour through her eyes. Yet the sordidness of the description reinforces one of the book's major themes – the 'health' (15) of the country as opposed to the town. We have been made fully aware in the preceding chapters that Fanny's personal health has suffered by her long residence in Portsmouth, and this has been caused by poor diet as well as lack of fresh air. In line 13 the sunshine is described as stifling, while in lines 15-16, we are shown that the atmosphere of the room is filled with particles of dust, and as for unhealthy diet, the milk (19) and buttered bread (20) are made as unappetising as possible. Fanny's health will not begin to improve until she returns to Mansfield. Towns are also unhealthy places from a moral point of view, and Fanny is about to receive news of immoral behaviour from London. Even Mr Price registers the fact that 'many fine ladies were going to the devil now-a-days that way' (57). The immorality of fashionable ladies is perhaps one of the 'stains and dirt' (14) that is brought out by sunlight in a city. Mary Crawford has already written that 'Varnish and gilding hide many stains', and her brother's and Maria's are about to be revealed.

Sunshine only serves to remind Fanny how much she is missing Mansfield. Indeed, her life has been made very enclosed by her present circumstances. Time has passed since her arrival, but only the position of the sun makes the change of season, and the scene she contemplates seems changed little from that of the first evening. Fanny seems to be almost mesmerised by what she is seeing, and the meticulously detailed and oppressive catalogue of the parlour is a remarkable piece of writing, not usually found in Jane Austen's fiction. No other passage in her novels comes near the sordid realism of this short passage, and yet some lines from it have a poetic quality, particularly 'the milk a mixture of motes floating in thin blue' (20) with its repeated vowels and consonants.

Fanny's reverie is accompanied by her mother's lamentations, which seem unending, and is finally broken by her father's question (26). Mr Price's speech is blunt, vernacular and dotted with oaths. It is amusing that of all the characters in the novel, he is the only one to take liberties with Fanny's Christian name (27) – the kind of fine detail we would expect of Jane Austen. We should also notice that Mr Price, like other naval officers in the novels, uses a number of nautical metaphors – on this occasion connected with the brutal punishments inflicted in the navy of the period (36–7).

Mr Price's method of encouraging a sense of morality in an erring daughter is harsh, but it serves to highlight Sir Thomas's failings as a father. The latter comes to believe, in the last chapter, that 'early hardship and discipline' have their advantages, and while few would wish for Mr Price as a father, many would concur that Maria's tragedy might have been avoided by the right kind of discipline. Once more, Jane Austen returns to one of her central themes by making us contemplate the parent–child relationship.

From the forthrightness of Mr Price's speaking voice the passage shifts effortlessly into the highly polished prose of the gossip column (38), which, like many of the period, deals in suggestion and innuendo. A careful reader has been partly prepared for the news of the elopement by the 'locked gate' episode at Sotherton, and by Mary's cryptic letter, but the sudden revelation of it in this unsuspected manner does come as a surprise to Fanny and reader alike.

Fanny's reaction is handled with great care. We are given the words she speaks on the instant – hesitant, repetitive – and then told what has been going on in her mind while they were being spoken. The sentence beginning line 49 is a model of construction. 'She spoke from the instinctive wish of delaying shame', is deliberately set against, 'she spoke with a resolution which sprang from despair', serving to highlight the contrary emotions that Fanny is feeling. A third phrase, 'she spoke what she did not ... believe herself', acts as an explanation, taking the shape of the other two by repeating 'she spoke', but emphasising the certainty of Fanny's conviction by the insertion of 'could not'. In a balanced way Jane Austen reveals that what her heroine says does not reflect what she believes. With other characters this might be used in an ironic fashion to suggest some kind of self-deception, but with Fanny it is the reaction of a delicate and sensitive mind that cannot even tolerate the notion of vice in others.

If Fanny's view is a little unworldly it is immediately and effectively countered by the lack of concern shown by her parents. Mr Price 'cared too little about the report' (55), while Mrs Price's plaintive but conventional cry of woe is silenced by the ironic revelation that the state of the carpet is giving her much more cause for concern (61). Her lack of any feeling is a family characteristic recalling Lady Bertram, who is also inclined to sit on a chair expecting others to do everything for her. Throughout the novel Jane Austen explores the similarities and contrasts in the characters and fates of the Ward sisters, outlined in the opening paragraph of Chapter 1.

This brief extract shows Jane Austen's talent at its best, observing minutely the social behaviour of a group of people. It is significant that one of the most dramatic events in the novel should take place out of the reader's sight, and be reported only at second hand. Vice is not a subject to be presented in full view in a Jane Austen novel, but its full implications are revealed by showing the effect it has on those who surround the offenders – on this occasion Fanny, and later Edmund. The comic and highly probable reaction of Mr and Mrs Price maintains the overall tone of the novel, which despite its central moral concerns, never loses sight of the everyday lives of men and women.

6 CRITICAL RECEPTION

6.1 CONTEMPORARY COMMENTS

Even while writing *Mansfield Park* Jane Austen was receiving critical
comments from members of her family. Her letters to Cassandra during
March 1814 report her brother Henry's comments from his first reading,
and it is clear that Cassandra herself has already read the manuscript.
Henry has enjoyed it, and praises the characters, particularly Lady Bertram
and Mrs Norris. He likes Fanny, and admires Henry Crawford as a 'clever,
pleasant man', though doubtless his admiration did not extend to Henry's
morals. According to Jane Austen, Henry found the last half of the novel
'*extremely interesting*'.

These comments, and others like them, must have proved enormously
valuable to the anonymous author, for after the book was published she
made her own collection, which can be found in the Macmillan Casebook
mentioned in the reading list. Most of the opinions are from relations or
family friends, but they show very diverse reactions, even though they are
primarily concerned with character and plot, and whether this new novel
measures up to preceding ones.

The character of Fanny proves the most controversial feature. Frank
Austen finds her 'delightful' and Edward approves as well, while his two
sons have opposed views – 'Edward admired Fanny – George disliked her.
– George interested by nobody but Mary Crawford'. One niece, Fanny
Knight, found the heroine to her taste, while another, Anna, 'could not
bear Fanny'.

The description of Lady Bertram and Mrs Norris was praised by several
people, and a Mrs Anna Harwood particularly enjoyed 'Mrs Norris & the
green Curtain'. Lady Gordon made the following perceptive comment
about the characters in general:

> In most novels you are amused for the time with a set of Ideal People whom you never think of afterwards or whom you the least expect to meet in common life, whereas in Miss A—s works, especially in MP you actually *live* with them, you fancy yourself one of the family . . . there is scarcely an Incident or conversation, or a person that you are not inclined to imagine you have at one time or another in your Life been a witness to, born a part in, & been acquainted with.

Much praise was also lavished by friends on the fidelity and power of the Portsmouth scenes.

Several commentators were annoyed by Maria's elopement with Henry, while Mrs James Austen found it 'very natural'. Mary Cooke, one of Jane Austen's distant relations, thought that Fanny 'ought to have been more determined on overcoming her own feelings, when she saw Edmund's attachment to Miss Crawford', while Ben Lefroy, a close family friend who was married to one of Jane Austen's nieces, was 'Angry with Edmund for not being in love with her [Fanny]'. Fanny Knight wanted 'more Love between her & Edmund - & could not think it natural that Edmund should be so much attached to a woman without Principle like Mary C (Crawford) - or promote Fanny's marrying Henry'.

It was obvious that *Mansfield Park* would be compared to *Pride and Prejudice*, but again opinions differed widely - 'We certainly do not think it as a *whole*, equal to P & P,' '. . .liked it better than P & P', 'not to be compared to P & P'. Cassandra 'thought it quite as clever, tho' not so brilliant as P & P'. Clearly, many were disappointed by the less sparkling nature of the new novel, but others were very impressed by its moral qualities, including the publisher Thomas Egerton.

What is interesting about these early comments is their very diversity, which would no doubt be reflected if a similar random survey were conducted today. They pinpoint the issues that have continued to fascinate critics into our own century, and have contributed to the notion that it is Jane Austen's 'problem' novel.

6.2 NINETEENTH-CENTURY CRITICS

Until the twentieth century *Mansfield Park* tended to be overshadowed by the other novels, but there were several important discussions of Jane Austen's work as a whole which helped to establish methods of approach that later critics would develop.

In 1815 Sir Walter Scott drew attention to the accuracy with which Jane Austen depicted ordinary men and women, and the fact that she concentrated on everyday events – 'the narrative of all her novels is composed of such common occurrences as may have fallen under the observation of most folks'. He argues that Jane Austen's kind of novel marked a new departure in that it avoided a craving after incident and an overemotional and sentimental effect on the reader.

Richard Whately in 1821, four years after Jane Austen's death, contributed an article to the *Quarterly Review* in which he praised *Mansfield Park*, for: 'It contains some of Miss Austin's [sic] best moral lessons, as well as her most humorous descriptions.' The moral aspect is considered in depth, particularly with reference to the upbringing of young ladies, and it is clear that Whately approves of Jane Austen's didactic purposes in writing: 'It is melancholy to reflect how many young ladies in the same sphere [as Maria and Julia Bertram], with what is ordinarily called every advantage in point of education, are so precisely in the same situation, that if they avoid a similar fate, it mut be rather from good luck than any thing else.' Whately also draws attention to the skill Jane Austen displays in creating female characters, and the sensitive way in which she handles Fanny's love for Edmund.

Another important critic was Richard Simpson, who wrote an article for the *North British Review* in April 1870. He argued that all Jane Austen's novels set out to teach: 'This didactic intention is even interwoven with the very plots and texture of the novel.' Simpson saw Jane Austen as a detached critic of society, using irony as a tool. He is particularly interested in the way she tantalises the readers of *Mansfield Park* into believing that Fanny and Edmund might have married their other choices:

> Yet she of course devotes all the machinery of the novel to bring together the true hero and heroine. Now, what is this other than taking a humourist's view of that which as a novelist she was treating as the summum bonum of existence? That predestination of love, that preordained fitness, which decreed that one and one only should be the complement and fulfilment of another's being. . . .

Simpson was one of the first critics to examine the way that certain themes appear throughout the major novels – in particular the analysis of married couples. The whole essay is well worth reading, and can be found in the Casebook mentioned above. Indeed, this single volume contains many of the important essays on *Mansfield Park*.

Modern critics have been as divided in their views as Jane Austen's first readers, and broadly speaking they may be separated into those who condemn the novel as uneven, and Fanny as 'priggish', and those who view it as a masterpiece because of the very qualities tht make it stand out from the other novels. The opposing views may be best illustrated by examining important essays by D.W. Harding and Lionel Trilling.

Harding's article first appeared in the literary journal *Scrutiny* in 1940, and has been reprinted many times. It is entitled *Regulated Hatred: An Aspect of the Work of Jane Austen*, and that alone is an indication of the way Harding views his subject. He rejects the notion that Jane Austen was a light, delicate humanist, and shows instead that her satirical comments are often directed at her readers, i.e. the society around her. She was aware of society's shortcomings, but out of respect for the virtues of civilised order, her attacks are disguised as comic – she offers 'her readers every excuse for regarding as rather exaggerated figures of fun people whom she herself detests and fears'. This comment could be applied to Mrs Norris.

The second half of the essay examines the 'Cinderella' theme which was mentioned in Section 4.1. At this point Harding launches into his attack on *Mansfield Park*. Fanny Price 'is the least interesting of all the heroines', because Jane Austen's emphasis is on 'the deep importance of the conventional virtues'. As a result the novel shows 'a distinct tendency to priggishness', and is 'a curiously abortive attempt at humility'. The section on *Mansfield Park* ends with the important point that Jane Austen winds up her plot, on this occasion, with surprising speed, as if she realised that the 'fairy tale' atmosphere was absurd.

Harding ignores many of the novel's subtleties, but his article certainly proved stimulating to critics who came after, and some first-time readers will find themselves sympathising with his condemnation of Fanny.

Among the critics who advocate the greatness of the novel, the most influential was Lionel Trilling, whose essay first appeared in *The Opposing Self* in 1954. Trilling argues that there seems to be little of Jane Austen's traditional irony in the novel. It asserts obvious truths and recommends all the virtues that modern readers find offensive – 'Yet *Mansfield Park* is a great novel, its greatness being commensurate with its power to offend.' In a wide-ranging argument Trilling outlines many important issues – Fanny's health, the fact that she is a 'Christian' heroine, the importance of a profession, the amateur theatricals, and the Crawfords. It is in connection with the latter that Trilling reaches the crux of his argument, that the irony in *Mansfield Park* is directed against irony itself, and in favour of 'hard literalness'. In her previous novels Jane Austen had shown that wit and vivacity were virtues, but in *Mansfield Park* these become a form of deceit - true virtue is to be found in plain speaking, or even awkwardness. Those readers who lament the absence of wit are missing the greatest irony in the novel.

Whether we totally agree with Trilling or not - and his essay has not discouraged further discussion from recent critics - his central point remains true, that *Mansfield Park* is great *because* it disturbs the way we think about the world around us, and the behaviour of our fellow men. A considerable amount has been written and published on the novel, but whatever professional critics say, it is one of those works of art that deliberately provokes us into thinking about important human issues, and does so while entertaining us.

REVISION QUESTIONS

1. 'The narrative of all her novels is composed of such common occurrences as may have fallen under the observation of most folks.' How far is this comment of Sir Walter Scott's applicable to the plot of *Mansfield Park*, and what are the implications of this?

2. 'Fanny Price is the least interesting of all the heroines' (D.W. HARDING). What are your own opinions on the heroine of the novel?

3. 'Mansfield is governed by an authority all too fallible.' Discuss this comment of Lionel Trilling's with particular reference to the characters of Sir Thomas and Mrs Norris.

4. Discuss the importance of everyday objects in the world of the novel.

5. 'God made the country, and man made the town.' (W. COWPER). What conflict do you find in the novel between urban and rural values?

6. 'Her light, bright, and sparkling comedy criticises while it diverts' (BARBARA HARDY). Examine three passages from the novel where comedy and criticism operate together.

7. With special reference to the visit to Sotherton (Chapters 9-10), discuss Jane Austen's ability to arrange characters into groups.

8. It has been said that the ending of the novel is too deliberately contrived. Would you agree or disagree with this view?

9. Show how the lives of the inhabitants of Mansfield Park are affected by the rehearsals for *Lovers' Vows*.

10. 'Jane Austen herself as narraor plays a . . . very large part indeed' (W.A. CRAIK). Outline what part you believe the narrator plays in the novel's structure.

FURTHER READING

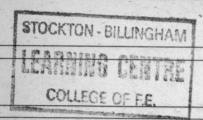
STOCKTON - BILLINGHAM

LEARNING CENTRE

COLLEGE OF F.E.

David Cecil, *A Portrait of Jane Austen* (London : Constable, 1978).

R.W. Chapman (ed.), *Jane Austen's Letters* (Oxford University Press 1932, revised edition 1959).

W.A. Craik, *Jane Austen: The Six Novels* (London: Methuen, 1965).

Barbara Hardy, *A Reading of Jane Austen* (London: Athlone Press, 1979).

F.B. Pinion, *A Jane Austen Companion* (London: Macmillan, 1973).

B.C. Southam (ed.), – *Jane Austen, Sense and Sensibility, Pride and Prejudice and Mansfield Park: A Casebook* (London: Macmillan, 1976).

R. Wirdnam (ed.), *Jane Austen: Mansfield Park* (London: Macmillan, 1984). (This text of the novel is specifically intended for those reading it for the first time.)